药品购销两票制政策透视

（中英双语版）

陈　昊◎著

科学技术文献出版社
SCIENTIFIC AND TECHNICAL DOCUMENTATION PRESS
·北京·

图书在版编目（CIP）数据

药品购销两票制政策透视：汉、英 / 陈昊著. —北京：科学技术文献出版社，2019.8
ISBN 978-7-5189-5859-7

Ⅰ. ①药… Ⅱ. ①陈… Ⅲ. ①药品—购销体制—研究—中国—汉、英 Ⅳ. ① F724.73

中国版本图书馆 CIP 数据核字（2019）第 165358 号

药品购销两票制政策透视（中英双语版）

策划编辑：周国臻　　责任编辑：宋红梅　　责任校对：文　浩　　责任出版：张志平

出 版 者　科学技术文献出版社
地　　址　北京市复兴路15号　邮编 100038
编 务 部　(010) 58882938，58882087（传真）
发 行 部　(010) 58882868，58882870（传真）
邮 购 部　(010) 58882873
官方网址　www.stdp.com.cn
发 行 者　科学技术文献出版社发行　全国各地新华书店经销
印 刷 者　北京虎彩文化传播有限公司
版　　次　2019 年 8 月第 1 版　2019 年 8 月第 1 次印刷
开　　本　787×1092　1/16
字　　数　206千
印　　张　10.5
书　　号　ISBN 978-7-5189-5859-7
定　　价　48.00元

前言

国务院常务会议在2016年深化医改重点工作安排中提出将全面推进公立医院药品集中采购，建立药品出厂价格信息可追溯机制，推行从生产到流通和从流通到医疗机构各开一次发票的“两票制”，使中间环节加价透明化。2017年，国家卫计委联合多个部委发布《关于在公立医疗机构药品采购中推行“两票制”的实施意见（试行）》，在全国范围全面实施药品购销“两票制”。至2019年6月，全国范围所有省（区、市）（港澳台地区除外）均已实现药品购销“两票制”，部分省（区、市）开始探讨将购销“两票制”相关政策借鉴推广至医用耗材领域。

在国家金税工程、深化综合医改、规范药品生产流通秩序、完善公立医院药品供应保障制度背景下诞生的药品购销“两票制”，作为一项重要的医药产业政策，全面调整和改变了我国医药流通领域的业务生态分布和价值链分配格局。在短期内，“两票制”极大压缩了医药流通环节中持续多年存在的非法购销和套现洗钱灰色空间，从源头上治理药品价格虚高现象，推动药品价格向真实价值回归；在中长期内，“两票制”将有助于强化药品生产企业或持证人的责任主体角色，规范其财税行为和营销方式，推动药品生产、流通行业回归本质，加速医药行业朝规范化、规模化、集约化方向整合。

本书撰写于上述背景下，是一部回顾、研究和系统分析药品购销“两票制”政策的专业著作，内容覆盖“两票制”政策的历史沿革、国家与地方版本具体方案、“两票制”核心政策解析、利益相关集团分析和政策理论依据与技术路线梳理等。

本书的读者对象为医药卫生体制改革、国家药物政策的研究与制定者，高等院校社会医学与卫生事业管理专业教学科研人员，医药生产流通领域管理者与决策人员，医药产业国内外投资者与行业研究人员等。鉴于药品购销“两票制”政策引起了国内外同行的广泛关注与深入研究，为促进与相关人士交流，本书采用了中英双语体例撰写。

笔者作为政策咨询专家，参与了相关部委和部分省市药品购销“两票制”政策的制定、起草和后期推行督导工作，对“两票制”政策有深入的认识和理解，期望通过本书的撰写与出版，与从事药品供应保障制度建设和研究的同道、同行进行充分的探讨、沟通与学习，共同推动对药品耗材购销“两票制”这一新生的药物政策的促进与完善。

在本书的出版过程中，学术秘书法国里昂商学院饶苑弘助理研究员承担了文字整理、校对工作，本书成稿亦得到武汉市深化医药卫生体制改革工作领导小组办公室副主任刘毅俊先生的指导与帮助，在此表示诚挚的谢意！

囿于本人学识有限与成稿仓促，书中难免存在诸多缺陷和疏漏，亦期待同行不吝批评与指正！

目　录

CONTENTS

在公立医疗机构药品采购中推行“两票制”是深化医药卫生体制改革、促进医药产业健康发展的重大举措，是规范药品流通秩序、压缩流通环节、降低虚高药价的重要抓手，是净化流通环境、打击“过票洗钱”、强化医药市场监督管理的有效手段，是保障城乡居民用药安全、维护人民健康的必然要求。

——《关于在公立医疗机构药品采购中推行“两票制”的实施意见（试行）》

一、政策背景与研究目标

（一）政策背景

药品购销“两票制”政策历史沿革如下。

“两票制”起源于地方医改实践，从2017年开始成为全国性的强制要求的医改重要政策，其发展轨迹可以概括为：缘起于广东，成型于福建，后全国燎原。

2007年，广东省公布了《广东省医疗机构药品阳光采购实施方案（初稿）》，第一次在省级政府文件中提出“两票制”概念。文件中表示“两票制”是为了简化药品领域采购流程，促进医疗机构药品采购行为规范化和医药企业有序竞争，以及建立公开、公平、公正的药品采购工作机制。有关部门希望通过竞价议价谈判使药品虚高价格降至合理价位；通过监管药品交易价格和票据流向，规范药品流通秩序，净化药品流通环境，促进医药行业健康发展；通过加强医疗机构用药情况监督，促进合理用药。同时，期望最终实现以下目标：推进药品购销监管的科学化和信息化建设进程，对药品购销全程实行有效监督，降低药品流通成本。在保证质量的前提下，通过公开竞价议价和价格谈判逐步形成医疗机构合理的药品采购价格。规范药品购销行为，推行阳光采购，实现药品采购全过程的公开、公平、公正，遏制药品流通领域违规违纪行为，纠正药品购销环节中的不正之风。

广东省药品挂网采购方案要求一级经销商必须直接从生产商购货、结算并开具发票，属转配送的，二级经销商必须直接从一级经销商购销结算，二级经销商的进项必须由一级经销商开具，此规定被业内人士概括为“两票制”。此后，由于药企和经销商共同反对，最终采购方案正式出台后，这一规定只是作为原则要求写进方案，在具体执行过程中，最多仍可实行“三票”，销售代理商作为特例获得合法地位。

2009年1月17日，卫生部、发展改革委、国家食品药品监督管理局等六部委发布《关于进一步规范医疗机构药品集中采购工作的意见》（以下简称《意见》），其中关于“减少药品流通环节”明确指出：药品集中采购由批发企业投标改为药品生产企

I. Policy background and research objective

(I) Policy background

The history of the Two-invoice System in the purchase and sale of drugs is as follows.

The Two-invoice System originated from the local medical care reform and had later become the important policy in the medical care reform mandatorily required nationwide from 2017. Its development trajectory showed that the development path can be summarized as it originated from Guangdong province, took shape in Fujian province and then spread to the whole country.

In 2007, the *Implementation Plan of the Sunshine Purchase of Drugs Among Medical Institutions of Guangdong province* (*first draft*) was released by Guangdong province, which for the first time proposed the concept of the Two-invoice System in a document at the provincial level. It indicated that the system was designed to simplify the purchase process of drugs, promote the standardization in the behaviors of the drug procurement among medical institutions and the orderly competition among them, and establish an open, fair and impartial drug purchase mechanism. Relevant departments hoped that we could reduce the drug price markups to the reasonable level through bidding, negotiation and discussion of prices; that we could regulate the sequence of circulation of drugs, purify the circulation environment for drugs and promote the healthy development of the pharmaceutical industry through supervising the transaction prices and the whereabouts of relevant invoices of drugs; and that we could promote the reasonable use of drugs through the strengthening of supervision on the use of drugs by medical institutions. Meanwhile, it was expected that the following goals will eventually be achieved: the scientific and informationalized construction process for the supervision on the purchase and sale of drugs will be promoted; and effectively supervising the whole process of the purchase and sale of drugs will be reducing the cost of drug circulation. The open bidding, negotiation and discussion of prices will be conducted under the precondition that the product quality is ensured so as to gradually form the reasonable purchase prices of drugs in the medical institutions. The purchase and sale of drugs will be regulated and the sunshine purchase will be implemented so as to realize the openness, fairness and justice in the whole process of the purchase and sale of drugs, curb any violation of regulations in the circulation of drugs and rectify any bad practices in the purchase and sale of drugs.

The proposal of the Procurement of Drugs by Means of Online Bidding in Guangdong Province requires that the initial distributors must directly purchase drugs from the manufacturers and settle the account with and issue the relevant invoices to them; where the drugs are used for distribution, the secondary distributors must directly purchase the drugs from the initial distributors, and settle the account with them, and the income of the secondary distributors must be invoiced by the initial distributors. This provision had been summarized as the Two-invoice System by the industry. Thereafter, due to the objection from the pharmaceutical enterprises and the distributors, the provision was only incorporated into the proposal as a principle after the final procurement plan was officially launched. During the concrete implementation process, the maximum can still be implemented “three invoices”, wherein the sales agents are granted the legal status as a particular case.

On January 17, 2009, the six ministries and commissions including the Ministry of Health,

业直接投标。由生产企业或委托具有现代物流能力的药品经营企业向医疗机构直接配送，原则上只允许委托一次。如被委托企业无法向医疗机构直接配送时，经省级药品集中采购管理部门批准，可委托其他企业配送。该《意见》为后来福建省实施药品购销“两票制”提供了国家层面的政策支撑。

2010 年 5 月，福建省在基本药物第七标全省集中采购中正式执行购销“两票制”，成为全国第一个实施“两票制”的地方省市。

2009 年 9 月 30 日，福建省食品药品监督管理局出台的《药品集中采购生产企业投标资质认定及管理办法》《药品集中采购药品配送企业投标资质认定及管理办法》《药品集中采购药品配送监督管理办法》（简称“三个管理办法”），为福建省“两票制”执行的具体政策措施。

三个管理办法规定：①中标生产企业可直接或委托片区内有配送资质的药品经营企业向医疗机构配送；②配送企业必须承担片区内所有实行药品集中招标采购的医疗机构的配送任务，不得跨片区配送（福建省药品集中采购全省划分为 10 个片区，即省属医疗机构单独 1 个片区、9 个设区市分别为 1 个片区）；③受委托的配送企业只能从委托的生产企业直接购进中标品种，非特殊情况，未经省药品集中采购领导小组办公室批准，不得从其他药品流通企业（含生产企业所属的流通企业）购进；④配送企业的配送费为药品中标价格的 5% ～ 8%，超过 8%，取消药品生产、配送企业的中标和配送资格，列入黑名单，取消下两个轮次的药品投标、配送资格。2010 年 5 月，福建省基药第七标药品集中采购正式执行“两票制”至今；2012 年 3 月，福建省非基药第八标药品集中采购继续执行“两票制”至今。

the National Development and Reform Commission and the State Food and Drug Administration promulgated the *Opinions on Further Regulation of the Concentrated Procurement of Drugs by Medical Institutions* (short for "The Opinions"), among which it clearly pointed out in the provision about "reduction of the circulation links of drugs" that "for the concentrated procurement of drugs, the bidding by a wholesale enterprise is changed to the direct bidding by a pharmaceutical manufacturer. The distribution of drugs should be directly conducted by the manufacturing enterprises or conducted by the drug operating enterprises with the modern logistical capability with the relevant entrustment; and in principle such entrustment could be made only once. If the entrusted enterprises fail to directly distribute drugs to the medical institutions, other enterprises could be granted such entrustment with the approval of the provincial management department in charge of the concentrated procurement of drugs." The Opinions provided policy support at the national level for the implementation of the later Two-invoice System in Fujian province with respect to the purchase and sale of drugs.

In May 2010, the Two-invoice System was officially adopted in the purchase and sale of drugs in a centralized manner in the whole province at the 7th bid for essential drugs, thus becoming the first province in China to implement the Two-invoice System.

On September 30, 2009, the Food and Drug Administration of Fujian Province launched the *Qualification Confirmation and Management Method of Manufacturing Enterprises Engaging in the Bid for Centralized Procurement of Drugs*, the *Qualification Confirmation and Management Method of Delivery Enterprises Engaging in the Bid for Concentrated Purchase and sale of drugs* and the *Supervision Management Method of the Distribution of the Drugs Purchased in a Concentrated Manner* (collectively called "Three Management Methods"). They were the concrete policies and measures for the implementation of the Two-invoice System in Fujian province.

The Three Management Methods specify that: ①the manufacturers which win the bid can directly distribute or entrust any drug operating enterprise with the qualification of operating the business of drugs within the area of its administration to distribute drugs to medical institutions; ②the distribution enterprises must undertake the task of distributing drugs to all medical institutions which are within its administration and purchase drugs in a centralized manner; however, such circulation enterprises should not conduct such distribution beyond specified areas (Fujian province was divided into ten areas for the centralized procurement of drugs, one single area for the provincial medical institutions, while nine cities consisting of districts form one area respectively); ③the entrusted delivery enterprises can only purchase the successful bidder varieties directly from the commissioned production enterprises; they should not purchase any drugs from other drug circulation enterprises (including the circulation enterprises affiliated with the manufacturers) under normal circumstances without the approval of the office of the leading group of the province in charge of the centralized procurement of drugs; ④the delivery costs incurred by the delivery enterprises are 5%~8% of the tender prices of relevant drugs; if the delivery costs more than 8%, the awarding of a bid and the qualification of distribution will be stripped from the manufacturers and delivery enterprises of relevant drugs; they will be put into the black list, and stripped of any qualification for bidding for and delivery of drugs for two rounds. The Two-invoice System was officially implemented in the centralized procurement of the 7th bid for essential drugs in Fujian Province in May 2010; and it was officially implemented in the centralized

福建“两票制”要求：药监部门每年数次对配送企业进行例行检查或专项检查，重点检查中标配送药品购进过程中的货单票同行的执行情况，即采购入库的药品品名、规格、剂型、数量、价格、金额；与中标药品生产企业开具的销售清单、销售发票上的相应内容是否完全一致；重点抽查销售环节中某一同批号药品的销售票据的对应情况；重点检查库存药品的进销存情况、仓库库存数量和电脑库存数量对应情况等。

福建“两票制”推行后，生产企业减少了药品流通环节，杜绝了挂靠、走票等违规行为，颠覆了药品个人代理商和没有配送资质的药品代理公司的原有操作模式，为中标生产企业重新整合市场，调整销售布局，完善销售网络建设，加强市场销售监管提供了良机；有强势品种或市场垄断地位的生产企业趁势实行了区域市场保证金、预付货款发货和现款发货制度；生产企业的片区商业的市场角色发生转变，销售数据下降，原分销和中转库功能丧失，只能代表生产企业做中标产品的各种商务工作，不利于片区发展；中标生产企业的销售数据急剧攀升，账面利润增加，纳税负担增大，如何处理好市场销售费用的返现问题，成为生产企业财务处理和税务处理的难题。生产企业的返现能力对中标产品特别是非基药产品的实际销量影响巨大。

同时“两票制”执行后，医院拖欠配送企业药款的情况没有改变，配送企业的回款周期变长。一般情况下，一批次药品销完后配送企业应安排回款，但很多时候回款时也会考虑医院的回款情况。因此，生产企业应收货款的资金沉淀会增大，风险也相应增加，如各片区的欠款大户几乎都是各配送企业。另外，部分低价的基药、非基药医院采购后退货频繁，迫使生产企业承担损失，生产企业的物流成本增加。全省配送分 10 个片区，配送商业多而且分散在各地；每个片区的销售情况不一样，大多数中标药品临床使用量小，难以做到批量采购和集中采购，因此，配送企业的采购计划频次多、数量少、金额低，导致生产企业发货的物流成本增加。

procurement of the 8th bid for essential drugs in Fujian Province in March 2012.

The Two-invoice System implemented in Fujian province required that the Drug Administration should conduct regular inspection or special inspection on the delivery enterprises for several times every year, with the focusing on checking the implementation of the practice of the goods accompanied with corresponding invoices during the procurement and distribution of drugs which win the bid, i.e. the names, specifications, dosage forms, quantity, prices and amounts of the drugs purchased and put in storage; on whether it is the same as the sales orders and sales invoices issued by the manufacturers which win the bid; on a spot examination on the correspondence of the sales bills for the drugs in the same lot number during the sales process; and on the correspondence of the purchase-sell-stock management of the stocked drugs, the quantity of the inventory in the warehouse and the quantity in stock stored in the computer, among others.

After the Two-invoice System was launched in Fujian province, the manufacturers had reduced the circulation links of drugs, thus completely eradicating such violations as an intermediary's being affiliated with a qualified drug business or the business of an intermediary which engaged in the business of drugs despite of its lack of relevant qualification. Consequently, it had subverted the original operating models wherein the individual agencies and agency companies of drugs could also engage in the distribution of drugs, thus providing an excellent opportunity for the reconstruction of the markets for the manufacturers which win the bid, the adjustment of the marketing arrangement, the perfection of the sales network and the strengthen of the marketing supervision. The manufacturers which possessed the advantageous varieties of drugs or a monopoly position in the market had taken advantage of the favorable situation in its implementation of the systems of the deposits for the regional markets, the payment in advance for dispatch of goods, and the delivery of goods subject to cash payment. The manufacturers had witnessed the change of their market role in the area of their operation, the decrease of sales data and the loss of their original functions of distribution and transfer warehouse; instead, they could only conduct all kinds of commercial work for the products which had won the bid, which was unfavorable to the growth of the areas of their operation. The manufacturers which won the bid had risen sharply; the book profits and the tax burden also increased. It had become a problem for the manufacturers in their financial transactions and tax treatment as to how they properly handled the returning of the payment for the marketing expenses. Actually, the capability of the manufacturers to return the payment had exerted a huge impact on the actual sales volume of the products which had won the bid, especially the non-essentialpharmaceutical products.

Besides, after the Two-invoice System was implemented, there was no change in the hospitals' default of the payment for the goods distributed by the delivery enterprises; furthermore, they suffered a longer cycle of the collection of payment. Generally, the delivery enterprises should arrange for the collection of payment after one batch of drugs was distributed; however, they had to consider the payment by the hospitals when they considered paying the manufacturers. As the result, the manufacturers would witness the increase of fund precipitation due to the failure to collect the payment for goods, along with the corresponding risks. For example, the major debtors in different areas under administration were mostly the delivery enterprises. Separately, part of the low-priced essential drugs and non-essential drugs were frequently returned upon procurement by the relevant hospitals, which

“两票制”的历史沿革如图 1 和图 2 所示。

2016 年 4 月 21 日，国务院办公厅发布《关于印发深化医药卫生体制改革 2016 年重点工作任务的通知》，要求综合医改试点省份在全省范围内推行“两票制”（生产企业到流通企业开一次发票，流通企业到医疗机构开一次发票），积极鼓励公立医院综合改革试点城市推行“两票制”，鼓励医院与药品生产企业直接结算药品货款、药品生产企业与配送企业结算配送费用。

2016 年 12 月 26 日，国务院医改办发布《关于在公立医疗机构药品采购中推行“两票制”的实施意见（试行）的通知》，进一步推动在公立医疗机构采购中推行“两票制”。

“两票制”给现有的药品采购及流通模式带来了变化，为医药生产企业、商业流通企业及医疗机构带来了挑战。对于生产企业而言，“两票制”意味着无法直接通过层层分包模式销售，商务团队将直接管理更多的供应商，并且部分省份实施“两票制”甚至“一票制”，商务团队还需应对不同的运作模式。“两票制”政策实施对生产企业各部门的保障能力提出了新的要求。首先，生产部门必须保质保量地保证中标药品的生产；其次，后勤部门必须及时准确安全地运输药品，销售清单、厂检随货同行，避免发货差错，减少运输破损，降低配送企业拒收及退货的风险；质管部门需保证电子监管码的及时上传及问题码的及时处理；最后，财务部门需及时开具销售发票并及时传递销售发票。对于医药流通企业而言，在药品购销“两票制”政策下，商业企业难以实现从省一级配送到全省所有医疗机构，尤其是小型流通企业，若不能符合大企业合规要求，将产生很大的合规风险。对医疗机构而言，甚至可能出现药物短缺风险。

2016 年，国务院发布《关于深化医药卫生体制改革 2016 年重点工作任务的通知》，将“两票制”的区域扩大到福建、上海、浙江、江苏、四川、青海、安徽和陕西 8 个省（市），同时获得重庆、辽宁、内蒙古、北京等地区的响应。其中明确提出：要构建药品生产流通新秩序，进一步完善药品生产质量管理规范和药品经营质量管理规范等政策体系，并严格监督实施；严格药品经营企业准入，规范药品流通秩序；严厉打击药品购销中的违法违规行为，预防和遏制药品、医疗器械与耗材采购中的不正之风

imposed relevant losses on the manufacturers, while they would suffer more costs in the logistics. The whole province consisted of ten areas for distribution, with the distributors in a great number and dispersed. There were different sales situations in all areas and it was difficult for most of the drugs which won the bid to be purchased in a batch or in a centralized manner due to the small quantities of their being used in clinical service. Hence, the delivery enterprises often met such procurement plans which featured high frequency, low quantity and low amount, thus causing the increase of the logistics costs for manufacturers.

The historical developments of tho Two-invoice System are shown in Figure 1 and Figure 2.

The General Office of the State Council released the *Notice of Printing and Distribution of the Key Tasks and Missions in 2016 for Deepening the Reform of the Medical and Health Sector* on April 21, 2016, requiring the provinces with the experiment units of the comprehensive medical care reform to launch the Two-invoice System, namely, an invoice which was issued for the process from manufacturers to circulation enterprises and an invoice for the process from circulation enterprises to medical institutions. It encouraged public hospitals in the cities which were selected as the experiment units for the comprehensive medical care reform to adopt the Two-invoice System; also, it encouraged the hospitals to directly settle accounts for drugs with the pharmaceutical manufacturers and the pharmaceutical manufacturers to settle the circulation expenses with the delivery enterprises.

The Medical Reform Office of the State Council released the *Notice on the Implementation Opinions on the Two-invoice System to Be Adopted in the Purchase of Drugs of Public Medical Institutions (for trial implementation)* on December 26, 2016, further promoting the Two-invoice System in the drug procurement of public medical institutions.

The Two-invoice System had brought changes to the existing drug procurement and distribution models and posted a challenge to the pharmaceutical manufacturers, commercial circulation enterprises and medical institutions. For the manufacturers, the Two-invoice System meant its failure to directly conduct sales which featured layer-by-layer subcontracting and the business teams would directly manage more suppliers. Moreover, part of the provinces had implemented the Two-invoice System or even the One-invoice System, wherein the business teams should still deal with different operating models. The Two-invoice System had raised new requirements for the guarantee capability of all departments of the manufacturing enterprises. First, the production departments must ensure the production of the drugs which have won the bid as per the required quality and quantity. Second, the logistics departments must timely, accurately and safely transport the drugs, along with the sales lists and inspection sheets by the manufacturers so as to avoid any errors in the shipments, reduce any damages in the transportation and reduce the risk of any rejection or returning of goods. The QC departments shall guarantee the timely uploading of the electronic monitoring codes and the timely handling of the problem codes. Finally, the financial departments shall timely issue and deliver the sales invoices. For the drug circulation enterprises, under the policy of the Two-invoice System in the purchase and sale of drugs, it is difficult for the commercial enterprises to distribute drugs from the provincial level to all medical institutions in the whole province; it is especially so for small circulation enterprises. If they fail to meet the compliance requirements of the large enterprises, there will be serious compliance risks. For the medical institutions, they may meet the shortage of drugs.

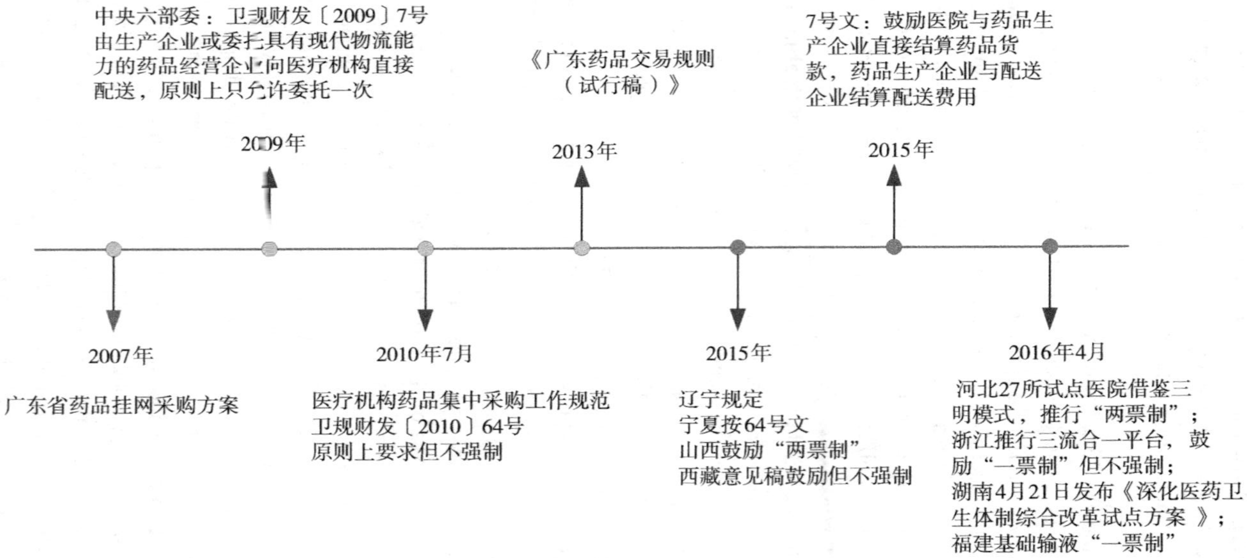

图 1　“两票制”的历史沿革 1

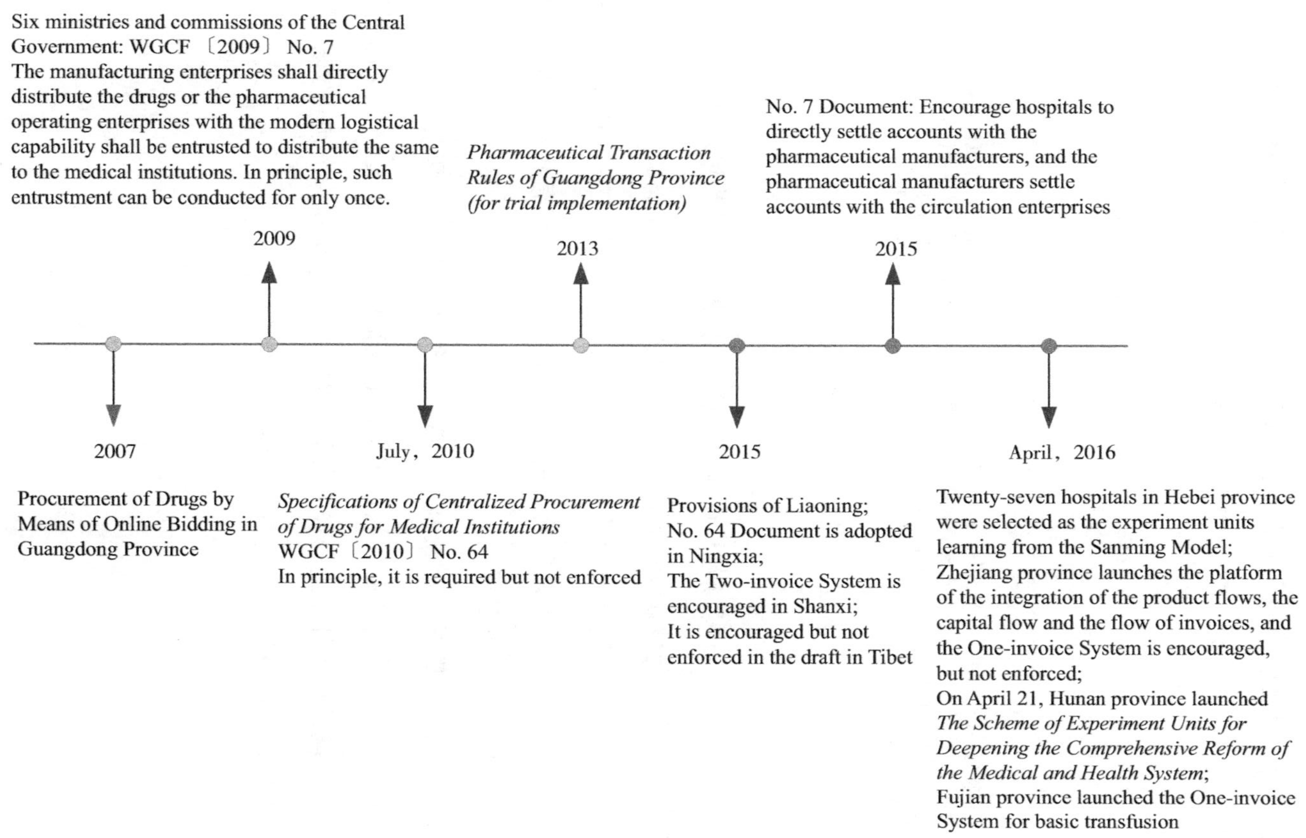

Figure 1　The historical development of the Two-invoice System (1)

和腐败行为；试行零售药店分类分级管理，鼓励连锁药店发展，组织医疗机构处方信息、医保结算信息与药品零售消费信息共享试点，推动医药分开。

2017年，国家卫计委联合多个部委发文《关于在公立医疗机构药品采购中推行“两票制”的实施意见（试行）》，在全国范围全面实施“两票制”。

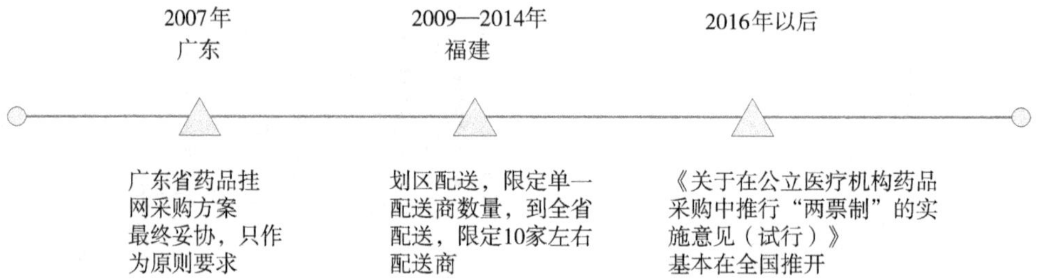

图2　“两票制”的历史沿革2

在上述背景条件下，本项目期望对“两票制”的实践展开较为详尽的研究，通过开展“两票制”政策分析与建议研究课题，梳理“两票制”政策背景，研究海外商业流通模式、国内各省市实施现状及相关方的运作模式，为合理实施“两票制”提出建议，支持国家级和省级卫计委合理实施“两票制”政策，同时也有利于优质、创新药品的商业流通，为患者带来更多权益。

本研究通过分析药品购销“两票制”政策背景和实施概况、“两票制”政策对医药行业的影响及药品购销“两票制”政策实施中的关键问题，探讨这一政策的创新与局限、值得总结有益经验及可以进一步完善的地方，以期寻找到一个切合实际、能够实现“两票制”的推行所设想的医改最终目标。

In 2016, the State Council released the *Notice on* the *Key Tasks and Missions in 2016 for the Deepening of the Reform of the Medical and Health Sector*, which specified that the Two-invoice System be expanded to Fujian, Shanghai, Zhejiang, Jiangsu, Sichuan, Qinghai, Anhui and Shaanxi, while responded by Chongqing, Liaoning, Inner Mongolia and Beijing, among others. It clearly proposed to construct the new order in the production and circulation of drugs so as to further improve the drug production quality management practice and the drug operation quality management practice, etc., and strictly supervise the implementation of them; restrict the access of drug operating enterprises and regulate the order of drug circulation; strictly punish the violations in the purchase and sale of drugs, prevent and curb bad practices and corrupt behaviors in the procurement of medical equipment and consumables; conduct the trial implementation of the management of drugstores in a classified and graded manner, encourage the development of chain drugstores, organize the experiment units of sharing the prescription information of medical institutions, billing information of medical insurance and retailing consumption information of drugs and push the separation of clinic from pharmacy.

In 2017, the National Health and Family Planning Commission joined hands with some ministries and commissions to release the *Implementation Opinions on the Two-invoice System to Be Adopted in the Drug Procurement of Public Medical Institutions* (*for trial implementation*), with an aim of implementing the Two-invoice System nationwide.

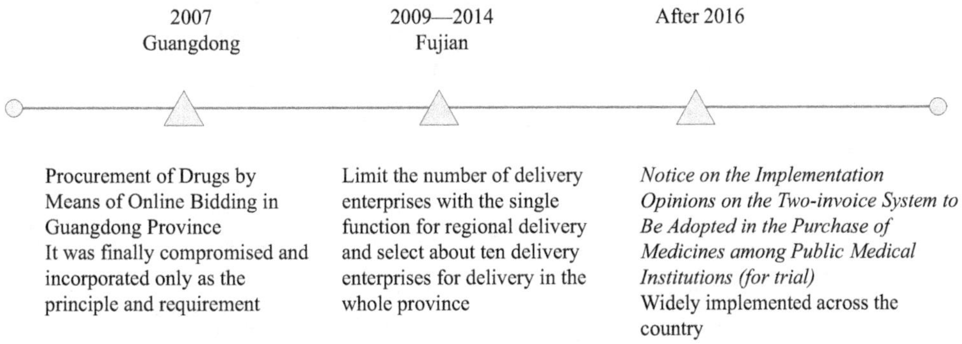

Figure 2 The historical development of the Two-invoice System (2)

Under the above background and conditions, this project expected to conduct a comparatively detailed research on the practice of the Two-invoice System; streamline the policy background of the System through conducting the policy analysis of and suggestions on the research topic on the System; and research the overseas commercial circulation models, the current implementation of the System in the provinces and cities in China and the operating models of relevant parties. It proposed suggestions on the reasonable implementation of the Two-invoice System and supported the health and family planning committees at the national and provincial levels in their reasonable implementation of the System; meanwhile, it was designed to be favorable to the commercial circulation of excellent and innovative drugs, thus bringing more benefits to patients.

By analyzing the policy background and the implementation survey of the Two-invoice

（二）研究目标

本研究期望通过对我国药品购销“两票制”的政策背景、历史沿革、现状进行系统化的理论研究，通过实证调查研究和开展利益相关者访谈，分析药品购销“两票制”实施对医药行业带来的影响，通过对药品购销相关理论与实践开展系统分析和专题讨论，探索建立有利于保障药品稳定供应、体现创新药品的药品购销“两票制”实施方法，保障患者及医疗机构选择使用创新药品的机会，并将研究成果与相关部门沟通和推广，提升研究成果的可行性，为完善我国药品商业流通体系提供支持。在上述研究的基础上，寻求合理表达医药行业立场并形成对政府相关部门的政策建议。

System in the purchase and sale of drugs, impact of the System on the pharmaceutical industry and the discussion about the key issues in the implementation of the System, this research discusses the innovation and limitation of this policy, the beneficial experiences worth being summarized and the places to be further improved so as to seek a final objective for the medical care reform which corresponds with the practical situation and can realize the Two-invoice System.

(II) Research objective

By the systematical and theoretical research on the policy background, historical development and current situations of the Two-invoice System in the purchase and sale of drugs in China, the empirical investigation and research and the interviews of the stakeholders, this research analyzes the impact of the implementation of the Two-invoice System in the purchase and sale of drugs. Through the systematic analysis and special discussion about the relevant theories and practice of the purchase and sale of drugs, it explores the implementation method of the Two-invoice System in the purchase and sale of drugs which is favorable to the stable supply of drugs, embodies the innovation of new drugs and protects the opportunities for the patients and medical institutions in their selection and use of new drugs; also communicates the research achievements with the relevant authorities and promotes them; and enhances the feasibility of the research achievements and provides supports for the commercial circulation system of drugs in China. On the basis of the above research, it strives to reasonably express the standpoints of the pharmaceutical industry and form the policies and suggestions for the relevant government departments.

二、研究内容与研究方法

（一）研究内容

（1）研究药品购销“两票制”政策背景、国家版本“两票制”文件和省市地方“两票制”实施、实践的概况。

（2）研究药品购销“两票制”政策对医药行业的影响，主要探讨对药品生产企业、药品流通及配送服务型企业的影响；医疗机构在“两票制”背景之下业务和行为方式变化的影响；以及上述利益相关者的行为应对预判。

（3）对药品购销“两票制”政策实施中的关键问题开展探讨，包括对“两票制”政策中关键的“票”的界定、验票方式和国家及省市“两票制”政策实施过程中引发的特殊情况进行解析。

（4）从政策定位视角对药品购销“两票制”进行政策分析，探讨基于上述分析，表达行业观点，并提出对政府相关部门的政策建议。

（二）技术路线图及相关思维导图

“两票制”技术路线图及相关思维导图分别如图 3 和图 4 所示。

II. Research contents and methods

(I) Research contents

(1) Research the policy background of the Two-invoice System in the purchase and sale of drugs, the national version of the documents concerning the System and the profile of the implementation and practice of the System in the provinces and cities.

(2) Research the impact of the Two-invoice System in the purchase and sale of drugs on the pharmaceutical industry and focus on the impact on the pharmaceutical manufacturers, the drug circulation and distribution service-type enterprises; the impact on the change of the business and behavioral patterns of the medical institutions in the context of implementing the Two-invoice System; and the response and prognosis of the above stakeholders.

(3) Discuss the key issues of the Two-invoice System in the purchase and sale of drugs, including the method of defining and inspecting the key "invoices" in the policy of the Two-invoice System, as well as the interpretation of the special occasions in the implementation of the Two-invoice System in the country as well as the provinces and cities.

(4) Analyze the policies of the Two-invoice System in the purchase and sale of drugs from the orientation and angle of policy. Based on the above analysis, it expresses the viewpoints of the industry and proposes the policies and suggestions for the relevant government departments.

(II) Technology roadmap and relevant mind mapping

The technology roadmap and relevant mind mapping of the Two-invoice System are shown in Figure 3 and Figure 4 respectively.

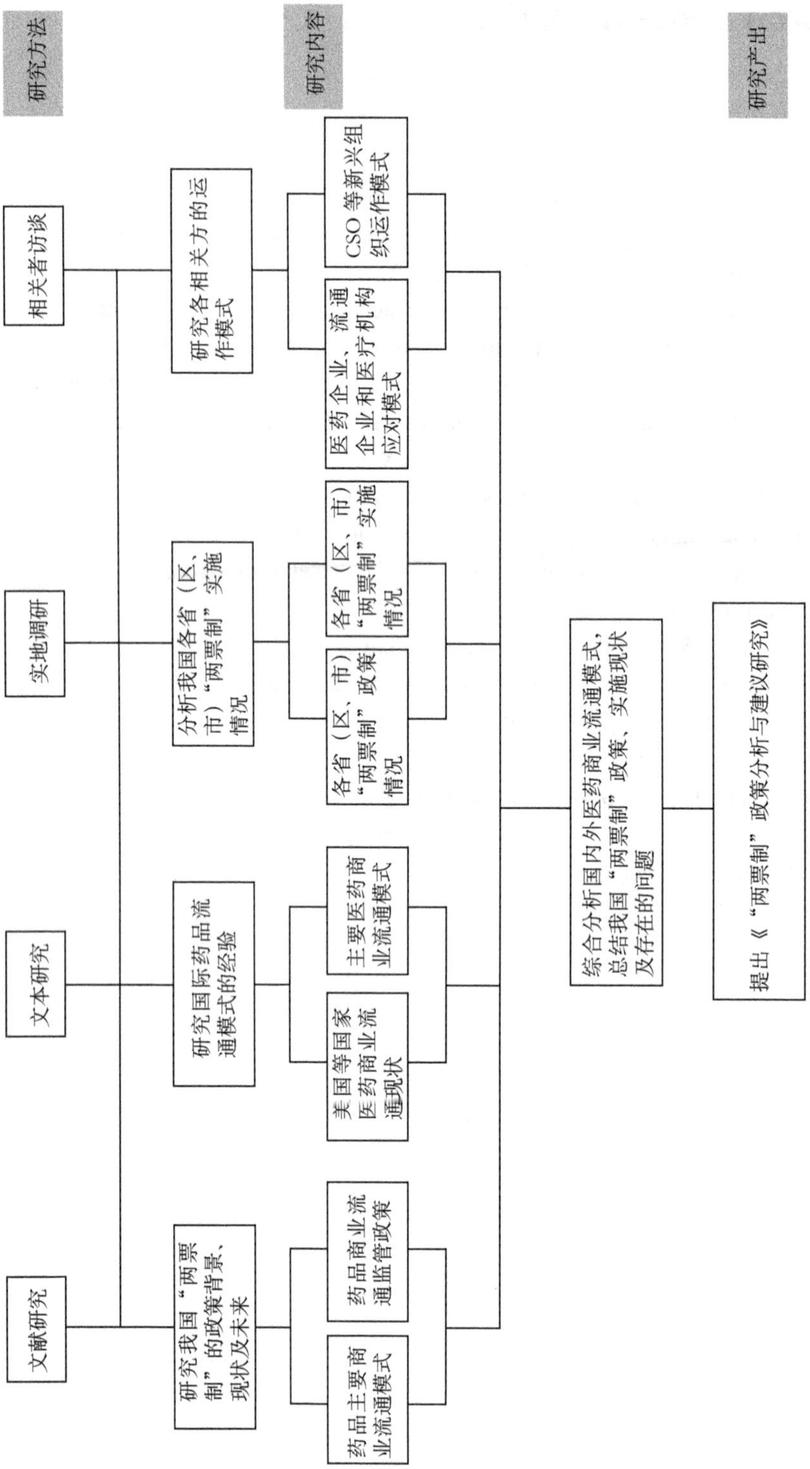
研究方法
文献研究
文本研究
实地调研
相关者访谈
研究内容
研究我国“两票制”的政策背景、现状及未来
研究国际药品流通模式的经验
分析我国各省（区、市）“两票制”实施情况
研究各相关方的运作模式
药品主要商业流通模式
药品商业流通监管政策
美国等国家医药商业流通现状
主要医药商业流通模式
各省（区、市）“两票制”政策情况
各省（区、市）“两票制”实施情况
医药企业、流通企业和医疗机构应对模式
CSO等新兴组织运作模式
研究产出
综合分析国内外医药商业流通模式，总结我国“两票制”政策、实施现状及存在的问题
提出《“两票制”政策分析与建议研究》

图3 “两票制”技术路线

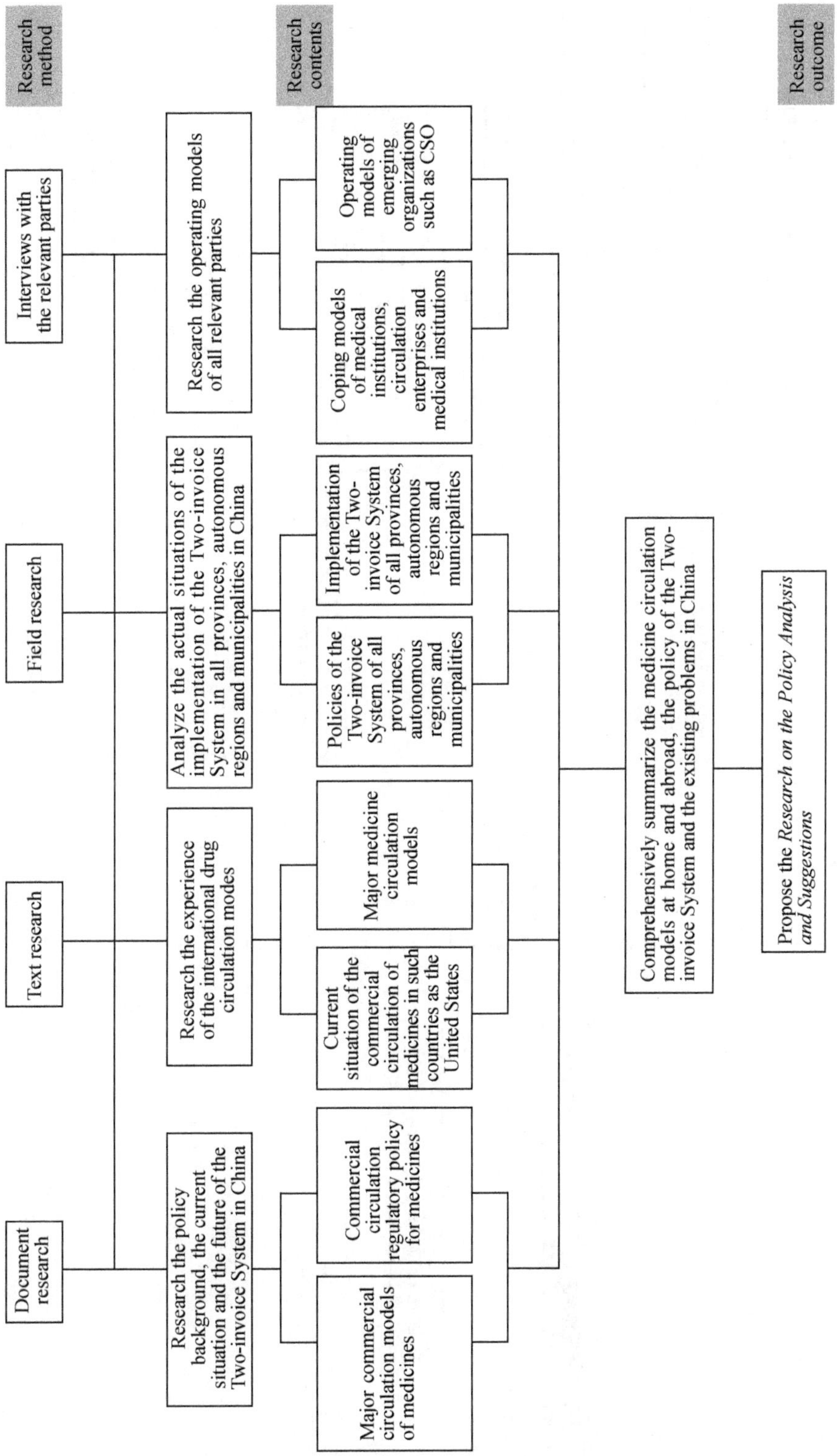

Figure 3 Technology roadmap of the Two-invoice System

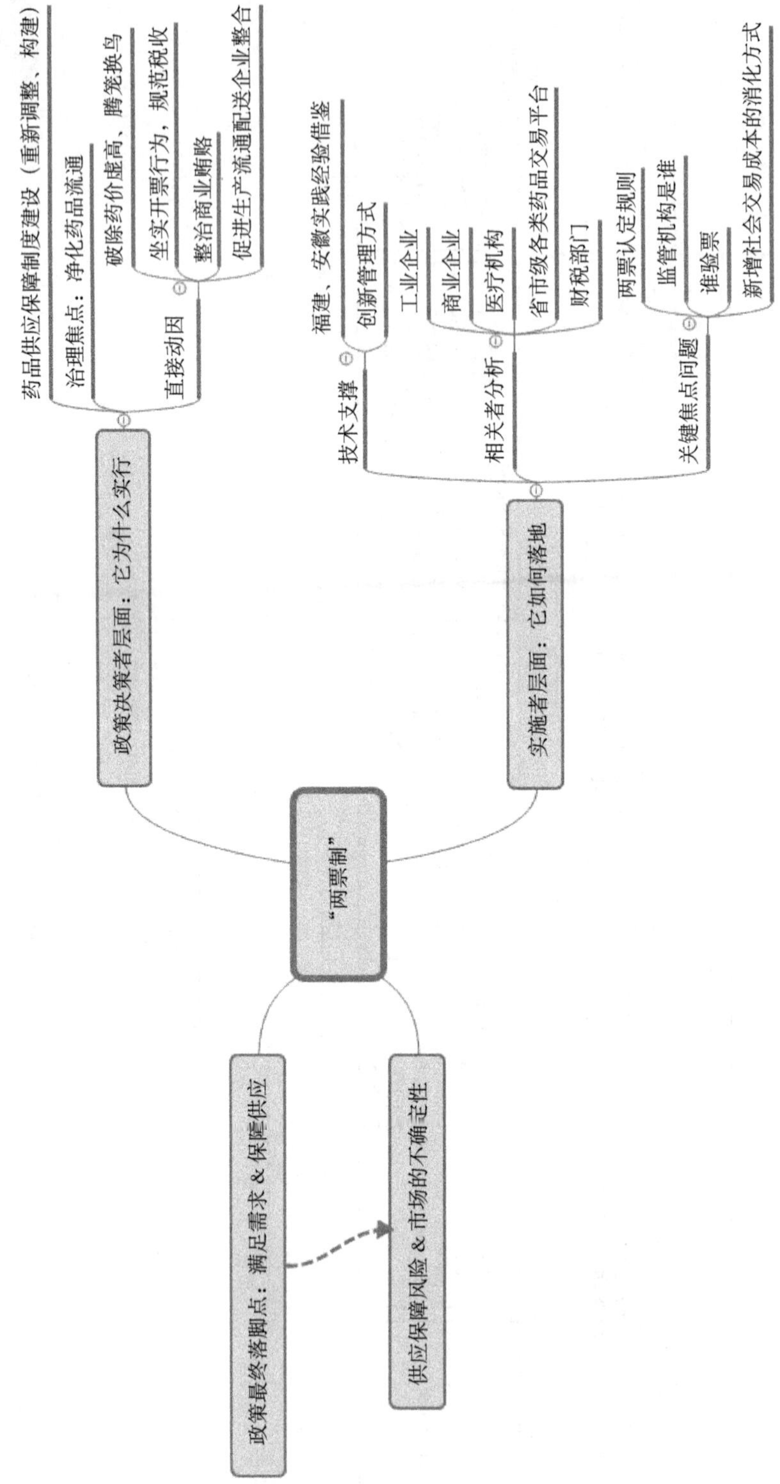

图 4 "两票制"相关思维导图

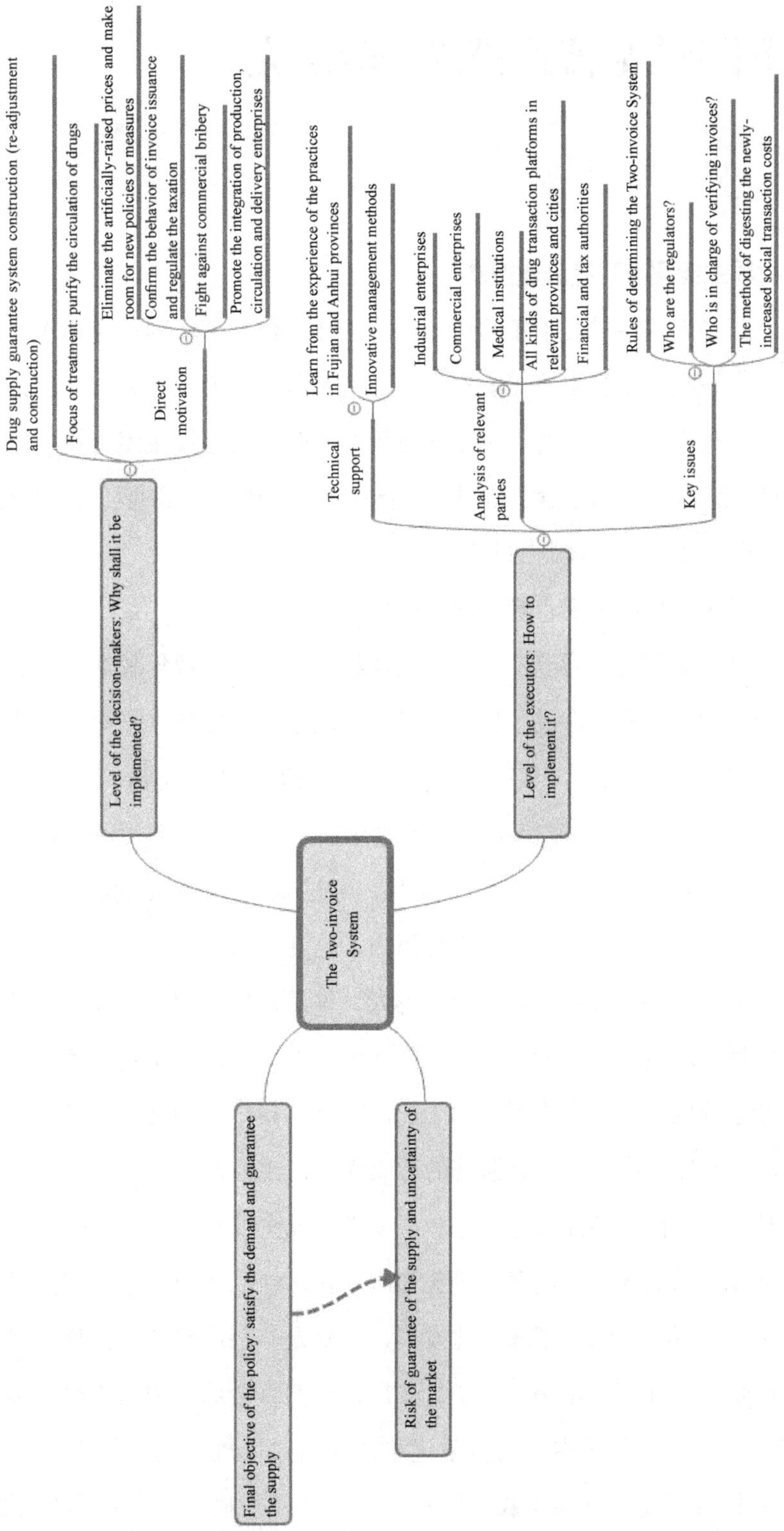

Figure 4 Relevant mind mapping of the Two-invoice System

三、国际药品流通模式经验研究

（一）世界主要国家药品流通模式

国外药品流通经过几十年的市场经济洗礼，药品市场和流通运作模式已经相当成熟和规范。在欧美及日本等发达国家和地区，医药物流企业大部分已经实现了规模化经营，市场集中度很大，特别是一些超级的医药物流连锁集团，在买方市场中起主导作用，排名前几位的连锁集团在市场中占到相对垄断地位，占据了绝大部分市场份额。

国外药品现代流通体制的共同特征如下。

1. 药品市场集中度高，竞争优势明显

在药品流通市场发展早期，流通企业相当多。经过数年长期激烈的市场竞争，企业联合、收购、兼并，形成了目前规模大、成本低、服务水平高的企业。德国目前只有 10 家大的药品批发商，其中 3 家最大的批发商占市场份额的 60% ～ 70%。在法国 8 家药品批发企业中，3 家市场份额高达 95%。美国前 3 家大型的药品批发企业的销售额占全美总销售额的 95% 以上。而且，经过 20 多年的激烈竞争，美国批发商数目减少了一半，而且基本转型为物流分销商，这几十家配送中心，为全美近万家药店和医院药房供应药品，其规模效益越来越大，虽然销售利润率在大幅下降，但费用率下降的速度远远超过了销售利润率下降的速度，大型物流分销商为美国药品流通过程中费用不断下降发挥了重大作用。由于药品市场的集中度相当高，这些国家对药品市场的监管非常有序且有效，而且监管的行政成本也比较低。

而且在发达国家药品流通体系中，大型批发企业处于垄断地位，优势明显，实行全球一体化的采购模式，经营连锁化和国家化。在欧美及日本等发达国家和地区，医药物流企业大部分已实现了规模化发展，特别是一些超级的医药物流连锁集团，大多属于跨国企业，在买方市场中起主导作用，他们在全球范围内进行大集团采购或药品联合采购，取得采购成本上的竞争优势，并通过大规模的招标极大地降低了采购成本，在原材料市场就开始了成本的战争，而且成效显著。一些小企业因很难独立维

III. Empirical research on the drug circulation models worldwide

(I) Drug circulation models in major countries worldwide

After decades of market economy, foreign drug market and circulation and operation models have become very mature and standard. In developed countries and regions such as Europe, the United States and Japan, drug circulation enterprises have achieved large-scale operation with large market concentration; in particular, some super drug circulation chain groups play a dominant role in the buyer' market; and the chain groups at the front places occupy the comparatively monopoly position in the market as well as the vast majority of the market share.

The common characteristics of the modern drug circulation system in foreign countries are as follows.

1. The high concentration of the pharmaceutical market with obvious competitive advantages

At the early stage of the drug circulation market, there existed a great number of drug circulation enterprises in foreign countries. After the fierce competitions for a long period over the past years, which witnessed the combination, acquisition and merging of enterprises, there formed some enterprises with large size, low cost and high service level. Currently, there are only ten large pharmaceutical wholesale companies in Germany, including three largest wholesale ones who occupy 60%~70% of the market shares. In the eight pharmaceutical wholesales enterprises in France, three occupy a market share as high as 95%. In the United States, there are three large pharmaceutical wholesale enterprises which occupy a market share as high as 95% or above. Moreover, after the fierce competitions for more than 20 years, half of the wholesale enterprises in the United States disappeared, and the rest have been transformed into logistics and circulation enterprises. The dozens of distribution centers provide drugs for nearly 10 000 drugstores and hospital pharmacies throughout the United States, with their scale becoming increasingly large. Despite of the substantial drop of their sales profits, the decrease of their expense ratio far exceeds the decrease of their sales profits. The large logistics and circulation enterprises have played an important role in the constant decrease of the circulation expenses of drugs in the United States. Due to the very high concentration degree of the pharmaceutical market, these countries could exert orderly and effective supervision on the pharmaceutical market, with the comparatively low administrative costs in the supervision.

Furtherly, in the drug circulation system in the developed countries, the large-scale wholesale enterprises occupy a monopoly position with obvious advantages. They adopt the procurement pattern featuring globalization as well as the chain-orientation and nationalization. In developed countries and regions such as Europe, the United States and Japan, most drug circulation enterprises have achieved large-scale development; in particular, some super drug circulation chain groups are mostly transnational enterprises. They play a dominant role in the buyer's market. They conduct large-sized procurement or united procurement of drugs worldwide, thus obtaining competitive advantages in terms of procurement cost; moreover, they have substantially lowered the procurement cost by means of large-scale bidding. In the market of raw materials, they start the wars of costs and got outstanding

持，而依附于大集团或者被并购。

2. 注重药品流通全过程的可追溯性和安全性

国外高度重视药品流通全过程的安全性和可追溯性。这主要表现在以下几个方面。

一是在全国进行销售的药品都有一个唯一的代码，相当于“身份证”，代码涵盖了药品的基本信息。例如，在美国，药品先通过FDA申请专利，成功后由NDC给予药品代码，然后才能进入销售环节。与此同时，药品批发和零售环节的包装都会有标准的条形码，这又涵盖了药品在不同流通环节的基本信息，因此，无论药品在何时何地销售给顾客，都很容易对其进行跟踪和追溯。

二是政府的监管制度也对流通过程的安全性和可追溯性做出了规定。美国FDA的监管制度，始终是以保障人民健康和生命安全为宗旨，以保证药物更加安全有效为监管主线，要求所有批发和零售商必须保存完整的交易记录，当某一个药品质量有问题时，可以即时地“追根溯源”。

3. 严格的市场准入制度

药品市场准入制度是指有关国家和政府准许公民和法人进入医药市场，从事药品生产活动的条件和程序规则的各种制度、规范的总称。药品市场准入制度作为保障药品安全有效的关键环节，在药品安全监管制度中具有极为重要的地位。发达国家一般都建立了严格的市场准入和认证认可标准体系。

4. 建立了现代物流配送体系，流通效率较高

国外形成了现代化的药品流通体系，流通效率非常高，这主要得益于药品流通过程的“三化”。

一是信息传输的先导化和网络化。欧美国家高度重视现代信息网络技术在药品流通中的应用。美国、日本的制药企业和批发商，都致力于推动医疗服务机构药品采购活动的信息化。在美国，药品经销企业为医疗机构和其他分销机构提供各种信息系统，包括订单处理、库存管理、决策支持、合同管理及处方调剂系统，以降低供应链成本。

二是产品标志的标准化。目前，欧美国家的每一种药品都有唯一的代码。与此同时，在所有药品销售包装上都有统一的条形码，这就为物流中心实现标准化、规范化、自动化拣选奠定了基础，大大提高了分拣速度，提高分拣的准确性。

achievements. It is very difficult for some small enterprises to maintain their business independence; instead, they have to rely on large groups or otherwise are merged or acquired.

2. Attach importance to the traceability and safety of the whole circulation process of drugs

Foreign countries attached great importance to the traceability and safety of the whole circulation process of drugs, which is shown in several aspects as follows.

Firstly, there is a unique code for each drug on sales in the whole country, which is equivalent to the "I.D. card" of the drug and covers the basic information of the drug. For example, in the United States, the patent of a drug should firstly be applied for through FDA, and the code therefrom would be granted by NDC, and then the drug could enter the sales section. Meanwhile, there are standard bar codes on the packages of drugs in the wholesale and retailing links, which cover the basic information of drugs in different links of circulation; hence, it is very easy to track and trace when and where drugs are sold to customers.

Secondly, the supervisory system of the government also specifies the safety and traceability of the circulation process. In the supervisory system of the United States, the protection of people's health and life is always taken as the principle and the guarantee of the safety and effectiveness of drugs as the main line in the supervision. All wholesale and retailing firms are required to keep the complete records of transactions. In case of any problem with the quality of a drug, the regulator could trace its roots immediately.

3. Strict market access system

The market access system of drugs refers to all kinds of systems and regulations wherein the relevant countries and governments allow their citizens or legal persons to access the pharmaceutical market and engage in the production of drugs. As the key link in the guarantee of the safety and effectiveness of drugs, the market access system of drugs occupies an important position in the drug safety regulation system. In the developed countries, the strict market access and certification and accreditation standard systems have generally been established.

4. Establish the modern logistics and distribution system, thus acquiring the comparatively high efficiency

In foreign countries, the modern drug circulation system has been formed, with a very high efficiency of circulation, which is mainly attributable to the networking, standardization and automation in the drug circulation process.

Firstly, it is the pioneering and networking of information transmission. The countries in Europe and Americas attach great importance to the application of modern information and networking technologies in the circulation of drugs. The pharmaceutical manufacturers and wholesale enterprises in the United States and Japan are all devoted to promoting the informatization in the procurement of drugs. In the United States, the drug distributors provide the medical institutions and other distributors with a variety of information systems, including the systems of order processing, inventory management, policy support, contract management and prescription and dispensing in order to reduce the costs of the supply chains.

Secondly, it is the standardization of product labeling. Currently, each drug has a unique code in Europe and Americas. Meanwhile, all sales packages of drugs are granted a unified bar code, which

三是物流过程的自动化。国外一些大型的药品流通企业都建立了自动化立体仓库，订单处理、拣货、补货、发货等主要作业项目都基本实现了自动化和智能化，大大降低了劳动程度，提高了工作效率。

5. 药品流通企业功能多样化

从传统意义上讲，美国的大型药品批发企业的业务通常是将从生产企业大规模购进的药品储存在自己的仓库中，然后再根据客户的需求，直接将药品销售给大型零售企业，如连锁药店、大型医院等。

最近几年，为了适应不断变化的市场环境，改变自己利润空间被蚕食的局面，批发商不断地扩大自己的客户链条。现在大型批发公司的客户几乎包括所有的卫生服务提供组织，主要包括：医疗中心、独立药房、连锁药店、其他的一些单位如诊所、小型卫生机构和全科医生诊所等。

6. 电子商务的推广与利用发展迅速

近年来，美国和欧盟地区的医药电子商务发展迅速，网上医药交易十分普遍。美国的药品网络交易增长迅速，不论是B2B类型的药品综合采购网（IDN），还是面向消费者B2C类型的药品网络零售，发展均十分迅猛。与此同时，基于信息化技术支撑的药品福利管理（PBM）和健康管理组织（HMO）均通过各种形式介入到药品电子交易体系内，提供管理控费和数据增值服务。

7. 形成较成熟的市场中间体和服务商

发达国家的医药生产和流通企业尊重企业之间的专业化分工，已经出现了比较成熟的药品流通市场中介组织。与药品流通相关的产品分类与编码、组织机构代码、数据通信服务、市场信息服务、企业信用服务等，都有专业化的市场中介组织为医药企业提供中介服务。这不仅大大降低了信息化的成本，而且提高了信息共享的程度，方便了网络的扩展。

与此同时，在美国和欧洲，医疗保健部门存在大量为医疗服务机构采购药品和医疗器械的集体采购机构。这些集体采购组织，作为医疗机构的利益代表，代表医疗机构与药品和医疗器械厂家谈判，签订合同，对医疗机构的经营和医疗成本有着重要影响。目前，美国几乎每一家医院都属于至少一个GPO（Group Purchase Organization, has laid a foundation for the realization of standardization, regulation and automation in the logistics centers, thus greatly enhancing the speed and accuracy of sorting drugs.

Third, it is the automation of the logistics process. Some large drug circulation enterprises abroad have set up their automatic stereoscopic warehouses; hence the major operating processes including order processing and sorting, supplementing and dispatching of goods are conducted in an automatic and intelligent manner. As a result, the labor intensity has been tremendously alleviated and the work efficiency greatly enhanced.

5. Functional diversification of drug circulation enterprises

In the traditional practice, large wholesale enterprises in the United States usually purchase drugs from the manufacturing enterprises in a large scale and store them in their own warehouses, and then directly distribute them to the large retailing enterprises, such as chain drugstores and large hospitals, as per the demand of them.

Over the recent years, the wholesalers have constantly expanded their client chains by adapting to the changing market environment and changing the situation that their profits were nibbled continually. Now the clients of large wholesale companies cover nearly all health care delivery organizations, mainly including medical centers, independent drugstores, chain drugstores and some other units such as clinics, small health agencies, GP surgeries and so on.

6. Fast promotion, use and development of e-commerce

In recent years, the United States and EU have witnessed the rapid growth of pharmaceutical e-commerce and the wide spreading of online drug trading. The United States saw the rapid growth of the online drug trading, including both B2B-type IDN for drugs and the B2C-type drug network retailing for consumers. Meanwhile, PBM and HMO which are based on the support information technology provide such services as management of expenses and value-added data by means of getting involved in the drug electronic trading system through a variety of forms.

7. Formation of comparatively mature market intermediaries and service providers

In the developed countries, the pharmaceutical manufacturing and circulation enterprises respect the division of labor based on specialization, and some comparatively mature intermediary organizations in the drug circulation market have emerged. There exist the professional intermediary agencies that provide intermediary service to pharmaceutical enterprises in respect of the product classification and coding, organization codes, data communication service, market information service, enterprise information service, etc., which are related to the drug circulation. This not only greatly reduces the cost of informatization, but also improves the degree of information sharing, thus to facilitate the expansion of the networks.

Meanwhile, in the United States and Europe, there exist a large number of collective procurement institutions which purchase drugs and medical equipment for medical institutions. These collective procurement organizations represent the interests of the medical institutions. They represent the medical institutions in the discussions with the manufacturers of drugs and medical equipment and the signing of contracts, thus exerting in important influence on the operating and medical costs of the medical institutions. At present, nearly all hospitals in the United States each have at least one GPO (Group Purchase Organization). More than 70% of the drugs for all hospitals are purchased by signing

简称 GPO）。所有医院的药品采购 70% 以上是通过 GPO 签订合同进行的，医疗机构每年利用 GPO 合同购买的药品和医疗器械价值为 1500 亿美元左右。GPOs 之间的规模不同，服务范围也不同。一般来说，GPO 的职责包括以下几点：①把采购能力集中起来增加谈判能力，获得折扣；②调查临床需要的产品市场代表；③医院协商供应并管理供应合同；④降低医院的运营成本；⑤简化购买程序并提高采购效率；⑥改进治疗的安全与质量。

（二）国外药品现代流通模式对我国的启示

从发达国家流通企业的发展轨迹和经验可以看出，商业企业必然要走扩大规模、降低成本这一集约化之路。考虑到我国药品流通的实际情况，流通领域不能完全照搬国外做法，应渐进改革，逐步到位。鼓励企业通过各种兼并、重组等方式扩大经营规模。与此同时，要考虑到在经济全球化背景下，医药商业企业的采购、仓储、销售、配送等协作关系日趋复杂，竞争已不单是产品性能和质量的竞争，还包括服务能力的竞争，因此，医药商业要加强与保健人群的沟通，满足客户对药品高效率运输的要求。

1. 实行医药分开，是构建药品现代流通体系的前提条件

在西方国家“医药分开”有着长远的历史，实践证明其对发展医疗技术，保证因病施治、合理用药，降低药费在医疗费用中的比例有效的。医药不分家容易扭曲价格机制对药品流向的调节作用，妨碍流通领域的正常竞争。部分过分追逐利益的医生可能会利用“开贵药、开多药”来获取高利润，这种做法严重损害了消费者的利益和医院的形象。使整个医药行业陷入混乱的局面。实施医药分开后，能够切断医院、医生与药品经营者之间的利益关系，促使药品行业朝着健康的方向发展。

美、法、德、日等国之所以药品流通且发展迅速，药品零售规模很大，主要也在于其医疗体制实现了医药分家。医药不分家容易扭曲价格机制对药品流向的调节作用，妨碍了流通领域的正常竞争。实施医药分开后，药品的主要销售渠道由医院转向批发、零售企业，极大地拓展了它们的生存与发展空间，打破医院的垄断地位，使消费者获得更多的知情权和选择权，利用市场机制和供求规律消除行业垄断。

contracts with GPOs. Every year, the medical institutions purchase drugs and medical equipment at the value of approx. 15 million U.S. dollars by means of such GPO contracts. There are different sizes in the GPOs, with different scopes of services. Generally speaking, the responsibilities of a GPO include: ① concentrate the purchasing power to increase the negotiation ability so as to obtain discounts; ② investigate the product market representatives required in the clinical services; ③ the hospitals coordinate the supply and manage the supply contracts; ④ reduce the operating costs of hospitals; ⑤ simplify the purchase procedure and enhance the efficiency of procurement; and ⑥ improve the safety and quality of medical treatment.

(II) Revelation of the foreign modern drug circulation models for China

From the development path and experiences of circulation enterprises in developed countries, we can see that it is essential for commercial enterprises to take the intensive way of expanding their business scales and reducing the cost. Given of the actual situation of the drug circulation in China, we cannot completely follow the practices of foreign countries in the field of distribution; instead, we should conduct gradual reform and achieve our goal in a gradual manner. We should encourage enterprises to expand their business scales by such means as a variety of mergers and recombination. At the same time, under the background of the economic globalization, the collaborative relations among medical businesses have become increasingly complicated in respect of their procurement, warehousing, sales and distribution, the competition not only concerns the performance and quality of products, but the competitiveness of the service ability; therefore, the medical businesses should strengthen the communication with the people who care for their health and fitness and satisfy the requirements for the high-efficient transportation at the places where the clients are located.

1. To separate clinic from pharmacy is the precondition for the construction of the modern drug circulation system

There was a long history of separating clinic from pharmacy in Western countries. Practice has proved that it is effective in the development of medical technologies, in the guarantee of treatment based on diseases and reasonable use of drugs and in the reduction of the proportion of expenses of drugs in the medical costs. On the contrary, the non-separation of clinic from pharmacy tends to easily undermine the role of the pricing mechanism in the adjustment of the flows of drugs, thus hindering the normal competition in the circulation domain. Some physicians may prescribe expensive drugs or overprescribe just to earn high profits. This practice has seriously harmed the interests of consumers and the image of hospitals, thus plunging the whole pharmaceutical industry into a chaotic situation. After the implementation of the separation of clinic from pharmacy, we can disconnect the interests relationship among the hospitals, physicians and drug operators, consequently promoting the pharmaceutical industry to develop in a healthy direction.

In such countries as the United States, France, Germany and Japan, the drug circulation had witnessed a rapid development, with the large-scale retail sale of pharmaceutical products. This was mainly attributable to the separation of clinic from pharmacy. The non-separation of clinic from pharmacy would easily undermine the role of the pricing mechanism in the adjustment of the flows of drugs, thus hindering the normal competition in the circulation domain. Upon the separation of clinic

2. 推进信息化、标准化，是构建药品现代流通体系的基础

美国、欧洲、日本等国家和地区的经验证明，药品流通体系创新的出路在于信息化、标准化建设，这是构建药品现代流通体系的基础工程。没有大规模的信息技术和信息平台，没有与之相匹配的标准，流通环节中各企业的协作就像沙滩楼阁，是无法建立和完成的。美国大型连锁企业成功运用 IT，给连锁药店带来了不可估量的价值。药品流通信息化支撑的基础又在于标准化的建设，这主要包括药品分类与编码、条形码、组织机构代码、企业和产品安全认证系统等，这极大地提高了药品流通的效率。最为重要的是，药品如果不进入物流配送体系，就不能进入市场，而药品如果不实行标准化生产和包装，就不能进入这个体系，这就使药品流通的安全性和可追溯性大大提高。

3. 提高药品市场集中度，是构建药品现代流通体系的可行路径

从发达国家流通企业发展轨迹和经验可以看出，商业企业必然要走扩大规模、降低成本这一集约化之路。考虑到我国药品流通的实际情况和存在“路径依赖”的现象，流通领域发展不能完全照搬国外做法。应渐进改革，逐步到位。鼓励企业通过各种兼并、重组等方式扩大经营规模，提高效率，发展一批跨地区、跨国的大型骨干企业集团。同时，要加大医药流通企业运用现代技术进行改造的力度，增加国家对流通技术研究、开发的投资和贷款，拓展建设资金来源，重点改造、建设一批大型药品批发、零售市场设施、物流配送中心、现代化仓储设施等，鼓励企业做大、做强、做优，改变我国药品流通费用过高、资金周转速度过低的局面，促进现代物流业的发展。

与此同时，要考虑到在经济全球化的背景下，医药商业企业的采购、仓储、销售、配送等协作关系日趋复杂，竞争已不单是产品性能和质量的竞争，还包括服务能力的竞争。

from pharmacy, the major distribution channels of drugs shifted from the hospitals to the wholesalers and retailing enterprises. This had tremendously expanded their space of survival and development, broken the monopoly status of hospitals, and granted more right to know and right of selection to consumers. In such way it used the market mechanisms and the law of supply and dem and to eliminate monopoly industries .

2. To push informatization and standardization lays the foundation for the construction of the modern drug circulation system

The experiences obtained in the United States, the European countries and Japan have proved that the outlet of the innovation of the drug circulation system rest with the construction of informatization and standardization. This is the fundamental project for the construction of the modern drug circulation system. Without the large-scaled information technology and information platform as well as the standards match therewith, the collaboration among all enterprises in the circulation sector would be like a pavilion on the beach, which is doomed to be a dream. The successful operation of IT in the large chain enterprises in the United States have brought inestimable value to the chain drugstores. The foundation which supported the informatization in the drug circulation lies in the construction of standardization. It mainly includes the classification and coding of drugs, bar codes, organizational codes and the enterprise and product authentication system, which have greatly enhanced the efficiency of drug circulation. The most important thing is that if the drugs have not entered the logistics and distribution system, they would not be able to enter the market. Meanwhile, if the drugs are not produced and packed in a standard manner, they would not be able to enter this system, which has significantly increased the safety and traceability of the drug circulation.

3. To enhance the concentration of the pharmaceutical market is feasible for constructing the modern drug circulation system

From the development trajectories and experiences of the circulation enterprises in developed countries, we can see that it is essential for commercial enterprises to take the path of intensification which features expansion of scale and reduction of costs. Given of the actual situation and the phenomenon of "path dependence" in the drug circulation in China, we should not completely follow the foreign practices in the development of the circulation domain. Instead, we should conduct reform and achieve the goal in a gradual manner. We should encourage enterprises to expand business scale, enhance efficiency and develop a batch of cross-regional or transnational large key enterprise groups by means of all kinds of M & A and recombination. Meanwhile, we should intensify the reformation of modern technologies among the drug circulation enterprises and increase the investment and loans of the State in the research and development of circulation technologies; moreover, we should expand the capital resources for construction and focus on the construction of a batch of large pharmaceutical wholesales and retailing facilities, logistics and distribution centers and modern warehousing facilities, etc. and encourage the enterprises to strive to become larger and stronger so as to change the current situation in China which features the overly high drug circulation expenses and overly low capital velocity speed. In such way we will promote the development of the modern logistics industry.

Meanwhile, considering the background of the economic globalization, the collaborative relations of the pharmaceutical businesses are becoming increasingly complicated in terms of

4. 规范企业经营行为，是构建药品现代流通体系的关键

长期以来，美、日两国的制药企业销售药品，主要依靠医药代表的促销活动。2001 年，日本制药企业共有医药代表 45 282 人，平均每 4 个医生就有 1 个医药代表。美国医药企业拥有的医药代表也有增长趋势，仅强生公司就拥有医药代表 6000 人。为了规范医药代表的促销行为，美、日两国的医药行业协会都制定了医药代表行为规范，规定了医药代表的职能和行为方式，要求医药代表必须通过医药协会组织的岗位培训和资格考试后持证上岗。日本的医药代表不需要具备医学或者药学专业学历，但必须系统接受医药代表专业培训，并参加医药代表资格考试。如果医药代表违法违规参与药品销售业务，采用不正当手段促销药品，一经发现，将被取消医药代表资格并终身不得从事医药代表业务。

procurement, warehousing, sales and distribution. The competition not only concerns the performance and quality of the products, but the competitiveness of the service ability.

4. To regulate the operation of enterprises is the key in the construction of the modern drug distribution system

For a long time, the sales of drugs by the pharmaceutical manufacturers in the United States and Japan were mainly reliant on the promotional activities by the medical representatives. In 2001, there were 45 282 medical representatives in the pharmaceutical manufacturers in Japan; namely, one representative was arranged for four physicians on average. In the United States, there was a trend of increase in the number of medical representatives in the pharmaceutical enterprises; for example, only Johnson and Johnson has 6000 medical representatives. To regulate the promotional behaviors of the medical representatives, the pharmaceutical profession associations in both the United States and Japan formulated the code of conduct for the medical representatives, specifying the functions and behavioral patterns and requiring that they must not take appointment with certificate until they have passed the on-the-job training and qualification test organized by the pharmaceutical profession association. In Japan, the medical representatives are not required to possess the education background of drug or pharmacy; however, they must accept the systematic and professional training for medical representatives and take the qualification test. If they violate any laws or regulations in the marketing of drugs, or they promote drugs by improper means, their qualification of medical representative will be stripped of once such violation has been found, and they are prohibited from engaging in any business of medical representation for the rest of their lives.

四、药品购销“两票制”政策相关释义

（一）“两票制”概念

药品购销“两票制”是指对公立医院集中采购的药品实施购销两张发票管理，药品生产企业到流通企业开一次发票，流通企业到医疗机构开一次发票。

药品生产企业或科工贸一体化的集团型企业设立的仅销售本企业（集团）药品的全资或控股商业公司（全国仅限一家商业公司）、境外药品国内总代理（全国仅限一家总代理）可视同生产企业。药品流通集团型企业内部向全资（控股）子公司或全资（控股）子公司之间调拨药品可不视为一票，但最多只允许开一次发票。药品生产、流通企业要按照公平、合法和诚实信用的原则合理确定加价水平。鼓励公立医疗机构与药品生产企业直接结算药品货款，药品生产企业与流通企业结算配送费用。

为应对自然灾害、重大疫情、重大突发事件和患者急（抢）救等特殊情况，紧急采购药品或国家医药储备药品，可特殊处理。

麻醉药品和第一类精神药品的流通经营仍按国家现行规定执行。

（二）“两票制”政策概要及实施过程

2017 年 1 月 9 日，国务院医改办会同国家卫生计生委等 8 部门联合印发《关于在公立医疗机构药品采购中推行“两票制”的实施意见（试行）的通知》（以下简称《实施意见》），要求综合医改试点省（区、市）和公立医院改革试点城市的公立医疗机构率先执行“两票制”，鼓励其他地区推行“两票制”。2017 年进一步扩大“两票制”实施范围，争取 2018 年在全国全面推开。

IV. Relevant paraphrasing of the Two-invoice System in the purchase and sale of drugs

(I) Concept of the Two-invoice System

The Two-invoice System in the purchase and sale of drugs means that two invoices are issued in the procurement and sales of the drugs which are purchased by public hospitals in a centralized manner: one invoice is issued to cover the process from the pharmaceutical manufacturers to the circulation enterprises and the other invoice to cover the process from the circulation enterprises to the medical institutions.

The wholly-owned or shareholding commercial companies that are set up by the pharmaceutical manufacturers or the group-type enterprises which integrate scientific research, manufacturing and trading and only engage in the sales of drugs manufactured by such enterprise groups themselves and the general agency in China for foreign drugs (only one such general agency is allowed for such foreign pharmaceutical enterprises in the whole country) can be regarded as the manufacturing enterprises. The allocation of drugs between the group-type enterprises of drug circulation and their wholly-owned (or shareholding) subsidiaries or that among the wholly-owned (or shareholding) subsidiaries of the group-type enterprises can be regarded as not covered by one invoice, but for the most one invoice can be issued. The pharmaceutical manufacturers and the circulations enterprises should reasonably set the price increase level in accordance with the principle of fairness, lawfulness and good faith. The public medical institutions are encouraged to directly settle the payment for drugs with the pharmaceutical manufacturers, and the pharmaceutical manufacturers should directly settle the circulation expenses with the circulation enterprises.

To deal with such special occasions as natural disasters, major epidemics, major incidents and first aid and rescue of patients, the emergent procurement of drugs or the national storage of drugs can be handled in a special manner.

The circulation and operation of narcotic drugs and psychotrophic substances Ⅰ should be handled as per the current provisions of the State.

(II) The policy outline and the implementation process of the Two-invoice System

On January 9, 2017, the eight departments, including the medical care reform office of the State Council and the National Health and Family Planning Commission of the People's Republic of China, jointly printed and distributed the *Notice on the Implementation Opinions on the Two-invoice System to Be Adopted in the Drug Procurement of Public Medical Institutions* (*for trial implementation*) (short for "Implementation Opinions"), requiring that the public medical institutions in the provinces (autonomous regions and municipalities) which were selected for the comprehensive medical care reform experiment and the cities which were selected as the experiment units for the reform of public

《实施意见》指出，药品生产、流通企业销售药品，应当按照发票管理有关规定开具增值税专用发票或者普通发票，发票的购、销方名称应当与随货同行单、付款流向、金额一致。流通企业购进药品，应主动向生产企业索要发票。公立医疗机构在药品验收入库时，必须验明票、货、账三者一致方可入库、使用，不仅要向配送药品的流通企业索要、验证发票，还应当要求流通企业出具由生产企业提供的进货发票证据，以便互相印证。鼓励有条件的地区使用电子发票，通过信息化手段验证“两票制”。针对一些特殊情况，《实施意见》做了特别规定。例如，为保障基层药品的有效供应，规定药品流通企业为特别偏远、交通不便的乡（镇）、村医疗卫生机构配送药品，允许在“两票制”基础上再开一次药品购销发票；为应对自然灾害、重大疫情、重大突发事件和患者急（抢）救等特殊情况，紧急采购药品或国家医药储备药品，可实行特殊处理。

按照《实施意见》规定，对不按规定执行“两票制”要求的药品生产企业、流通企业，将取消药品集中采购投标、中标和配送资格，并列入药品采购不良记录；对索票（证）不严、“两票制”落实不到位、拖欠货款、有令不行的医疗机构要通报批评，直到追究相关人员责任。

在国家版“两票制”政策颁布施行之后，包括医改 11 个试点省在内，全国大多数省（区、市）陆续出台了省级“两票制”政策（及意见征集稿）。

自此，药品购销“两票制”政策成为药品生产流通领域一项重要的基本政策。

hospitals should take the lead to implement the Two-invoice System and that other areas should promote the System. In 2017, the scope of implementation of the Two-invoice System was furthered expanded and the System should be fully carried out across the country in 2018.

The Implementation Opinions pointed out that when marketing their drugs, the pharmaceutical manufacturers and the circulation enterprises should issue VAT invoices or common invoices as per the relevant provisions of the invoice management and the names of the purchasers and sellers on the invoices should be consistent with the bills accompanying the goods, the flows and amounts of payment. When purchasing drugs, the circulation enterprises should initiatively demand invoices from the manufacturing enterprises. When inspecting drugs and admitting them into warehouses, the public medical institutions must not put them into warehouses or use them until it has been proved that the invoices, goods and accounts are in consistent. They should not only demand and examine invoices with the circulation enterprises for the distribution of drugs, but require the circulation enterprises to issue the invoice evidences for the purchased goods as provided by the manufacturing enterprises so as to corroborate each other. The areas with sufficient conditions are encouraged to use electronic invoices and verify the Two-invoice System by means of information tools. For some special occasions, the Implementation Opinions had made special provisions: for example, to guarantee the effective supply of drugs at the grass-roots communities, it specifies that the drug circulation enterprises should distribute drugs to any medical and health organizations at the towns and villages which are remotely located and thus inconvenient accessible. In such cases, a drug procurement and sales invoice is allowed to be issued on the basis of the Two-invoice System. To deal with such special occasions as natural disasters, major epidemics, major incidents and first aid and rescue for patients, as well as the urgent procurement of drugs or the national storage of drugs, some special measures can be taken.

In accordance with the provisions of the Implementation Opinions, any pharmaceutical manufacturers and circulation enterprises which fail to implement the Two-invoice System will be stripped of the qualification of tendering, winning of the bidding and distribution of drugs which are purchased in a centralized manner, and be included in the record of bad behaviors in respect of drug procurement. A notice of criticism will be circulated for the medical institutions which are not strict with invoices or vouchers, fail to implement the Two-invoice System, default in payment for goods and do not take relevant instructions, till the relevant personnel will be investigated and claimed against their corresponding responsibilities.

Upon the promulgation and implementation of the Two-invoice System of the national version, most provinces, autonomous regions and municipalities in China, including the 11 provinces which were selected for the experiment of the medical care reform, successively launched the provincial-level policy of the Two-invoice System and the drafts thereof.

Ever since then, the Two-invoice System in the purchase and sale of drugs has become an important fundamental policy in the domain of pharmaceutical production and circulation.

五、实施药品购销“两票制”政策的医改背景、产业环境和技术条件梳理

（一）医改背景

1. 改革路径

随着我国社会经济发展水平的快速提高，医保、医疗、医药事业高速发展，我国医药卫生体系所采取的“医药合业、以药补医”的体制安排风险日益暴露、各种矛盾日益尖锐。一方面，和全世界所有成熟国家体系一样，我国社会面临人口老龄化、慢性病等造成沉重社会负担的疾病谱变化问题，民众的健康期望和卫生服务需求随着社会经济发展则不断提高，民众对医疗医药服务的渴求几乎趋于无限；另一方面，科学水平不断快速发展、医药技术不断进步，带来新的治疗手段、呈现新的治疗效果；同时，医学活动本身对价格昂贵的新技术和新药的使用大幅增加，则为社会和支付体系带来沉重的经济压力，几乎所有的医保支付体系都面临可持续安全运行的危机，控费、提效成为全球所有支付体系共同面对的难题。我国覆盖全民的基本医保体系的基本特征是“低筹资、广覆盖、低水平”，同样需面对上述艰难的局面。而我国的医药卫生体制同时还面对另外一项深层次的矛盾，即沿袭计划经济年代对医疗服务的价格管制并人为压低价格，使得医疗服务价格无法体现其专业价值。医疗机构和医务人员无法依靠提供优质的医疗服务获得专业发展所必需的体面收入，体制安排医疗机构通过药品价格加成获取收入来以药补医，支持医疗事业发展和医生获取富有争议的报酬。医药产业长期低水平重复生产、恶性竞争，同时普通药品价格受到管制，“微创新、伪创新”药品则能通过虚高定价获取较大的价格空间，这个价格空间再通过扭曲的营销结构和行为用于灰色促销。在“医药合业、以药补医”的体制安排下，产生医药合谋现象，医药价值链上几乎所有人的行为高度扭曲，医疗机构和医生过度用药、过度医疗，引发严重的医学后果和社会后果。医药费用持续高速增长，对医保制度长期安全、可持续运行形成沉重的压力，对民众医药费用增添沉重的经济负担，红包、

V. Systematize the background, industrial environment and technological conditions for the implementation of the Two-invoice System in the purchase and sale of drugs

(I) Background of the medical care reform

1. Path of the reform

With the rapid social and economic development in China and the high-speed development of the medical insurance, medical care and pharmacy sectors, the policy of "combining medical treatment with drugs and supplementing medical treatment with drugs" adopted by the medical and health system in China has exposed its defects and risks, along with the increasingly sharp contradictions of all kinds. On the one hand, just like all mature systems in the developed countries, the Chinese society is also faced with the problems of the changes of disease spectrum such as aging of population and chronic diseases which has brought about heavy social burdens. Meanwhile, the people's expectation for health and demand for health care service has kept enhancing along with the social economic development; moreover, their longing for the medical and pharmacy service seems to be unlimited. On the other hand, the fast-developing scientific level and the progress of the medical technologies have brought about new treatment methods and demonstrated new treatment effect. Meanwhile, the medical activities are in increasingly demand for new technologies and drugs which are usually expensive, thus creating heavy economic pressure on the social and payment systems. Nearly all medical insurance systems are faced with the risk of whether the sustainable and safe operation could be attained. Consequently, the control of charges and the enhancement of efficiency have become the difficulties commonly faced by all payment systems across the world. In China, the basic feature of the basic medical health insurance system covering all people is "the low level of fund collection, broad coverage of people and low level of treatment service", which is also faced with the difficult situation mentioned above. Moreover, the medical and health system in China is also faced with another serious contradiction; namely, the price control prevalent in the period of planned economy has been carried on and the prices are kept down artificially, enabling the medical service prices to be unable to embody its professional value. As a result, the medical institutions and the medical staff could not which obtain the necessary and dignified income for their professional development by means of providing excellent medical service; hence, medical institutions which obtain income through medicine markups achieve the goal of "compensating medical treatment with drugs". In such way we can support the development of the medical undertaking and encourage physicians to earn the disputed income. In the long time, the pharmaceutical industry have suffered from the low-level repeated production and vicious competition. Meanwhile, the prices of common drugs were controlled, while the micro-innovative and falsely-innovative new drugs reaped comparatively high value through the bubble prices. This bubble price space was applied in the gray promotional activities by means of the distorted marketing structure and behaviors. Under the institutional arrangement of "combining medical treatment with drugs and supplementing medical treatment with drugs", there occurred the phenomenon of contriving for profits between the medical

回扣盛行，极大地败坏了社会风气，并形成医患关系严重对立。公立医院扭曲的收入补偿机制造成医疗机构、医务人员、医药行业行为严重扭曲，由此产生医疗医药领域种种不正常现象，甚至会危及社会稳定运行。

基于上述原因，自 2015 年，在对 2009—2014 年深化医改取得巨大成就进行总结的同时，在医改部门主导下继续推动深化医改朝深水区迈进，即社会和学界称为“三医联动”驱动下的综合医改。

长期以来，我国医药卫生事业发展采取“医药合业、以药补医”的体制安排。虽然在特定历史阶段促进了医药卫生事业快速发展，但也为“看病难、看病贵”的顽疾埋下了体制性成因，极大地损害了道德价值观和社会总体福利。自 2009 年启动的第三轮深化医改，选择改革公立医院药品采购方式、整肃和重建医药生产流通秩序作为综合医改的切入点和突破口，期望通过压低公立医院药品价格和费用，为医疗服务价格调整提供改革空间，从而转变“医疗服务价格长期人为扭曲压低”所形成的公立医院补偿机制扭曲局面，从深层次解决我国医药卫生领域价值链分配失当、医疗医药行业普遍存在行为扭曲、医药费用增速长期居高不下的顽疾。

通过公立医院药品采购以实施药品购销“两票制”，压缩过多和相对无序的商业流通环节，可以视作降低药品流通成本、倒逼破除药价虚高的有益探索尝试，它的局部试点成效，也确实显现了这项改革措施的有效性与合理性。

与此同时，我国医药行业目前面临如下问题：医药工业发展减速，药品主仿制缺创新；医药商业发展放缓，运营压力较大；医疗器械主占低端市场，产品同质化严重；医疗服务资源供求不均，人才瓶颈等。要一一解决这些问题，必须调整医药行业产业结构，而“两票制”就是突破口。健康产业的供给侧改革已悄然启动，医疗的分级诊疗、医保的三保合一、支付方式改革、一致性评价、“两票制”等，将共同改变供给侧结构，影响未来的发展方式和增长效率。其中，“两票制”的推广，改变的不仅仅是流通领域，也事关健康产业整体改革进程。

institutions and the pharmacy sector. In the medical value chain, nearly all people were distorted in their behaviors and medical institutions and physicians tended to overprescribe, consequently producing the adverse medical and social consequences. The sustainable and high-speed increase of medical expenses had formed heavy pressure on the long-term safety and sustainable operation of the medical insurance system and caused heavy economic burdens on the people in terms of medical expenses. Moreover, the red packets and rebates were prevalent, greatly corrupting the social morality and forming serious contradictions between doctors and patients. The distorted income compensation mechanism in public hospitals had resulted in the serious distortion of the behaviors of medical institutions, medical personnel and the pharmaceutical industry, which in turn produced various abnormal phenomena in the medical treatment and drug sectors, or even endangered the stability of the society.

Based on the above reasons, since 2015 the medical care reform has been deepened under the guidance of the medical care reform authority while the huge achievements in the medical care reform were made during the period from 2009 to 2014. This is called the comprehensive medical care reform driven by the interaction of medical insurance, drug and medical treatment in the society and the academic circles.

For a long time, the institutional arrangement of “combining medical treatment with drugs and supplementing medical treatment with drugs” had been implemented in the development of the medical and health undertakings in China. Although it had facilitated the rapid development of the medical and health undertakings at the special historical stage, it formed the institutional cause for the chronic problem of “being difficult and expensive to get medical services”, consequently undermining the moral values and social overall welfare. The third-round in-depth medical care reform was implemented in 2009, wherein the reform of the drug procurement method by public hospitals and the rectification and reconstruction of the medical manufacturing and circulation order were selected as the entry point and the breakthrough in the comprehensive medical care reform, expecting to provide room of reform for the adjustment of the medical service prices by means of reducing the drug prices and costs in public hospitals so as to shift the distorted situation of the compensation mechanism of public hospitals which had been formed due to the reason that “the medical service prices has all along been kept down in an unreasonable manner”. In such way the chronic problem that there existed the improper allocation in the value chain in the medical and health domain in China, the prevailing distorted behaviors in the medical and health sectors and the long-term high-speed increase of medical expenses had been substantially solved.

The Two-invoice System has been implemented through the purchase and sale of drugs in public hospitals and the excessive and comparatively chaotic commercial circulation links has been eliminated. They can be regarded as the positive exploration and trial in the reduction of the circulation costs of drugs and the elimination of the price markups in a reverse manner. Such exploration and trial proved some success and has actually demonstrated the effectiveness and rationality of the reform measures.

Meanwhile, the pharmaceutical industry in China is currently faced with the following situation: the development speed of the pharmaceutical industry slows down and the drugs are mainly reliant on copying, but lack of innovation; the pharmaceutical business development slows down and the

此前福建、广东等省份试点“两票制”，期望还原药品销售过程中的真实价格，防止过票、洗钱、税收流失和制止医务人员收取回扣等商业贿赂。福建省三明市在三医联动的综合医改试点中，通过大力推行最低价采购、“一品两规”、“两票制”等改革措施，有力地降低了当地药价和药品费用，从源头上堵住药价虚高、商业贿赂盛行的问题，医药领域的行业风气得到极大净化，并为医改相关配套措施的顺利推行创造了良好的条件。三明市实施“两票制”的成效全国瞩目，并得到国家医改部门的肯定。在深化医改、扩大医改试点省份及城市数量、各地纷纷总结宣传和复制三明市医改经验的背景下，“两票制”在国务院常务会议层面表态实施，可以视为国家有关部门从政策层面对福建实践经验的肯定。“两票制”全面推行成为政策必然。

2. 药品供给侧改革

我国自 20 世纪中叶起，建设了以化学仿制药为主体的现代药品工业和以中成药现代剂型为主体的中医药工业及以基础疫苗为主体的生物制药工业，实现了大部分化学仿制药原料药的自给自足，并能生产大多数临床常用药品制剂。门类基本齐全的医药工业为满足国内医疗事业临床需求、改善我国卫生状况、提升居民健康水平做出了巨大贡献。

operational pressure is comparatively large; the market is dominated by low-end medical equipment and there are serious problems of product homogeneity; and there exists the problems such as the uneven supply and demand of medical service resources and the bottleneck of talented people. To solve these problems, we must adjust the structure of the pharmaceutical industry and the Two-invoice System is the breakthrough. On the other hand, the supply-side reform of the health industry has commenced unconsciously; the practices such as the classified diagnosis and treatment, the integration of the basic medical insurance of urban workers, the medical insurance of urban residents and the new-type rural cooperative medical insurance, the reform of the payment methods, the consistency evaluation and the Two-invoice System, among others, will combine to change the supply-side structure and affect the development methods and the growth efficiency in the future. The Two-invoice System has not only changed the circulation domain, but influenced the overall reform process of the health industry.

The Two-invoice System was experimented in such provinces as Fujian and Guangdong, aiming to restore the authentic prices of drugs during their sales process, prevent such commercial bribes as the business featuring the improper use of invoices issued by the pharmaceutical enterprises, money laundering, loss of taxes and prevent the medical personnel from collecting rebates. In its comprehensive medical care reform as an experiment unit which featured the interaction of medical insurance, drug and medical treatment, Sanming City in Fujiang Province has greatly reduced the local drug prices and costs by means of vigorously implementing such reform measures as the minimum price procurement, two kinds of provisions for one drug and the Two-invoice System. Moreover, this measure had solved the problems of the price markups and prevalent commercial bribes from the sources, significantly purified the industrial ethos of the drug domain and created excellent conditions for the promotion of the supporting measures related to the medical care reform. The achievements made in the implementation of the Two-invoice System in Sanming of Fujian had attracted the attention of the whole country and was accepted by the medical care reform authority of the State. Under the background that the medical care reform has been deepened, the number of provinces and cities selected to be the experiment units for the medical care reform has been increased and all relevant provinces and cities summarized, publicized and duplicated the experiences of the medical care reform in Sanming City, the Two-invoice System was implemented as per the solution as passed at the executive meetings of the State Council; therefore, the Two-invoice System can be regarded as the experience in Fujian as accepted by the relevant departments of the State from the level of policy. It is inevitable for the Two-invoice System to be comprehensively implemented.

2. Supply-side reform of drugs

Since the middle of the 20th century, China has built its modern pharmaceutical industry focused on generic drugs, the traditional Chinese drug industry focused on the modern dosage forms of Chinese patent drugs and the bio-pharmaceutical industry focused on the basic vaccines, thus realizing the self-sufficiency of most of the bulk chemicals for chemical generic drugs. Moreover, we can manufacture most of common clinical drugs and preparations. The pharmaceutical industry which basically featured a complete category has made great contribution to satisfy the clinical demand, improve the health conditions and enhance people’s health level in China.

但随着社会和经济水平日益发展，我国旧有的“医药合业、以药补医”体制逐渐暴露出巨大的缺陷。这一卫生体制安排又部分源自我国医药产业长期以来低水平重复生产、市场恶性竞争，同时药品价格长期处于管制状态而导致正常的市场竞争失灵，医药产业不得不寻求以从事“微创新、伪创新”为特征、谋取药品虚高定价，再通过非正常的生产流通体系安排来套取资金费用，用于临床和消费终端的非正常竞争这一扭曲的产业现状。由此，三医联动驱动的综合医改选择了“破除药品价格虚高，降低药品价格，从而降低药品费用，将医疗机构内通过药品谋取的收入比重降低下来，腾挪出来的空间用于调整医疗服务价格，从而重建公立医院的收入补偿机制”这一改革路径，纠正医药、医疗近乎全行业全员高度的行为扭曲。

2015 年，根据《关于完善公立医院药品集中采购工作的指导意见》（国办发〔2015〕年 7 号），全国范围以省为单位开展对药品实行分类采购，主要的采购方法是价格谈判和双信封招标。目的是通过大幅简化医疗机构用药目录、压缩药品剂型和品规、合并过于繁复的质量层次，来大幅降低公立医院药品价格，从而服务于深化公立医院改革。在此过程中，药品集中采购部门压缩药品供应中的质量层次的想法遭遇到现实挑战，即国内仿制药品质量与疗效不足，无法形成对相对昂贵的过专利期药品的价格压力和有效替代。如果进行仿制药替代，则可能引发临床用药风险和优质药品供应短缺；如果不进行替代，则又无法有效形成药品行业整体降价的压力。

在此背景下，2015 年下半年，以“药品临床试验自查风暴”“仿制药质量和疗效一致性评价”“药品医疗器械审评审批制度改革”为代表的药品供给侧改革举措陆续出台，改革文件的发文单位从国务院办公厅到国家食品药品监督管理总局，政策调整涉及修订药品管理法、药品注册管理办法等重要法规，形成延续至今的药品治理供给侧改革。

据相关数据，近年来我国医药产业产值虽然总量保持稳步上升，但增速自 2012 年下降以来一直呈明显走低态势。这自然与我国整体经济下行，医药产业自身总量已较为庞大，增幅比例有限等有关。另据南方医药经济研究所发布的数据，目前我国滞销药品的市场容量高达 800 亿元，药品滞销率约 3%。一方面，我国人口老龄化趋势加剧，伴随生活水平提高，居民医疗保健和药品支出需求增加；另一方面，医疗资

With the increasing development of the society and economy, the original system in China which featured the combination of medical treatment and drugs and the supplementing for medical treatment by drugs has gradually exposed a significant defect. This institutional health system partly originated from the long-term low-level repetitions in the production and the vicious market competition in the pharmaceutical industry for a long period of time in China. Meanwhile, the drug prices had been long under control, thus resulting in the failure of the normal market competition. In such circumstances, the pharmaceutical industry had to seek for solutions to the distorted industrial situation which featured the micro-innovation and false innovation in the development of drugs which sought for the overly-pricing of drugs and extracted funds and charges for the clinic and consumer end by means of abnormal production and circulation systems. Hence, the comprehensive medical care reform driven by the interaction of medical insurance, drug and medical treatment had selected the path of reform which aims to “eliminate bubble prices or lower drug prices so as to reduce drug expenses, decrease the proportion of the income obtained through drugs within medical institutions and adjust medical service prices, thus reconstructing the income compensation mechanism in public hospitals”; hence, we will be able to rectify the highly distorted behaviors of almost all the participants in the pharmacy and medical industries.

The classified drug procurement was implemented across the whole country with provinces as the units in 2015 in accordance with the *Guiding Opinions on the Improvement of the Centralized Procurement Plan of Drugs of Public Medical Institutions* (GBF〔2015〕No. 7), the main method of procurement being the price discussion and the winning of the envelope bidding. The purpose was to substantially reduce drug prices in public hospitals and thus serve the in-depth reform of public hospitals by means of greatly simplifying the medication catalogue in medical institutions, decreasing drugs and dosage forms and combining with the overly complicated quality levels. In this process, the idea of the departments in charge of the centralized procurement of drugs of decreasing the quality levels in the supply of drugs met challenges; namely, there was a lack of quality and curative effect of generic drugs, thus failing to form the price pressure and effective substitution for the drugs which were comparatively expensive and passed the patent life. If we use generic drugs as substitutes, we may cause the risk in the drugs in the clinical use and the shortage of supply of excellent drugs; but if we do not develop the substitutes, it will be impossible for us to effectively form pressure on the overall drug prices.

In such context, the supply-side reform measures of drugs represented by “the storm of self-check on the clinical researches on drugs”, “the consistency evaluation of the quality and curative effect of generic drugs” and “the appraisal and approval institution reform” were launched successively in the second half of 2015. The documents of reform were released by such departments as the General Office of the State Council through the China Food and Drug Administration, with the adjustment of policies covering the revision of the food and drug administration and the drug registration management measures, among others; thus the supply-side reform of drugs which lasts till now has been formed.

As the relevant data showed, the recent years saw the stable increase of the total output of the pharmaceutical industry in China; however, its growth has showed an obvious downward trend all the way since 2012. This is naturally related to the overall economic downturn, the already massive total

源和药品信息不对称，药质与药价不对称等导致行业预期产值和效益水平难有上行空间。在国家倡导供给侧改革的大环境下，医药产业若要升级发展，需在伴随总需求扩大的同时，着力提高供给体系质量和效率。2016 年两会期间《政府工作报告》提出推进医疗、医保、医药联动改革，对我国医药行业的总体布局做出较全面的梳理；3 月 11 日，国务院正式出台《关于促进医药产业健康发展的指导意见》（国办发〔2016〕11 号），提出仿制药、国产药、国产医疗器械、医药现代物流、中药标准、智能医疗等相关的一系列指导政策。

3. 价格政策

长期以来，我国药品价格规制失灵、药价虚高、服务价格失真。政府及主管部门将治理药价虚高、遏制“大处方”泛滥作为重要的改革目标，相应制定多项价格干预政策，但效果始终差强人意。

2015 年 5 月 5 日，国家发展与改革委员会颁布实施《关于印发推进药品价格改革意见的通知》（发改价格〔2015〕904 号），我国药品价格管理开始转型。药品价格政策从直接干预具体价格，转变为重点监督管理药品价格行为、防范垄断和不正当竞争，并确定市场机制是药品价格形成的主要机制，医保药品价格主要是通过制定实施医保支付标准的方式间接引导形成。

我国药品生产流通领域所存在的长期顽疾包括：药品生产领域低水平重复严重、市场恶性竞争，大多数工业企业采取“底价包销”的方式进行销售；流通环节则参与者众多，“挂靠、走票”“无证经营”等违法现象严重，过多过滥的流通环节通过虚列开支、套取税收差异、偷逃税款等形式套取现金，用于药品销售终端环节（包括医院和社会药房）不道德促销。

amount of the pharmaceutical industry and the limited growth proportion. Separately, according to the data released by the Southern Medicine Economic Research Institute, the current market capacity of unsalable drugs in China reaches as high as 80 billion yuan, with the unsalable rate of about 3%. On the one hand, the trend of the aging of population in China has intensified; and with the improvement of people's livelihood, there has been an increasing demand for expenditure for health care and drugs. On the other hand, there exists the imbalance of the information between medical resources and drugs, and the asymmetry between the drug quality and the drug prices and other factors. They combined to make it difficult to obtain any space for the increase of the expected output and benefit level of the industry. In the macro-environment wherein the State advocated the supply-side reform, if the pharmaceutical industry required any upgrading and development, the quality and efficiency should be increased in the supply system while expanding the overall demand. During NPC and CPPCC of 2016, the *Government Work Report* proposed to push the interactive reform of medical care, medical insurance and pharmacy and conduct a comparatively comprehensive systemization of the overall arrangement of the pharmaceutical industry in China. On March 11, the State Council officially launched the *Guiding Opinions on the Promotion of the Healthy Development of the Pharmaceutical Industry* (GBF〔2016〕No.11), proposing a series of guiding policies relevant to generic drugs, domestic drugs, domestic medical equipment, modern drug circulation, traditional Chinese drug standards and intelligent medical care, among others.

3. Price policy

For a long time, there has existed the failure of regulating drug prices, the drug price markups and service price markups. The government and its competent departments take the treatment of the drug price markups and the suppression of the abuses of "large prescriptions" as the important reform goals and correspondingly formulated multiple price intervention policies, but the result is far from being satisfactory.

On May 5, 2015, the National Development and Reform Commission promulgated and implemented the *Notice of Printing and Distributing the Opinions on the Promotion of the Drug Price Reform* (FGJG〔2015〕No. 904), commencing the transformation of drug price management in China. The drug policy shifted from the direct intervention of concrete prices to the focus on supervision and management of the drug price behaviors and the prevention of monopoly and unfair competition. It also determined that the market mechanism is the major mechanism of forming the drug prices and that the prices of the drugs within the medical insurance system should be formed indirectly under the guidance of the medical insurance and by implementing the payment standards under the medical insurance.

The problems existing in the drug production and circulation domain for a long period of time in China include low-level serious repetitions in drug production field and vicious market competition, most of industrial enterprises adopting the method of "exclusive sales at floor price" in the marketing. In the circulation sector there exist such violations as numerous participants, "affiliation and the business of an intermediary which engages in the business of drugs despite of its lack of relevant qualification" and "unlicensed business operation". There have been excessive circulation links which illegally withdraw cash to be used in the immoral promotional activities at the terminals of drug sales (including hospitals and drugstores in the market) by such means as artificially listing expenditure,

药品购销“两票制”，期望规范并约束药品从生产、流通到医院终端的流通次数来规范药品购销行为，压缩、简化流通环节，从而破除药品价格虚高现象，实质性地降低药品价格，服务于综合医改的政策目标，同时实现对药品行业的规范治理。

通过实行购销“两票制”，减少药品流通环节，一方面达到控制药品价格的目标；另一方面，促进药品生产流通行业整合，淘汰过多的非规模经济商业公司，净化流通环境，从而促进医药产业健康发展。

回顾历史，从2006年药品加成以实际购进价为基础，顺加不超过15%的加价率作价后，医药费用不降反升。在全面实施“药品零差率”之前，我国药品定价机制采用的主要是顺价作价定价机制，但在信息严重不对称的药品市场，企业掌握有关药品研发、生产、管理的各项成本信息，处于绝对的信息优势地位。而政府规制机构却缺乏对药品生产各项成本的确凿信息，处于信息劣势地位，药企通过虚报各项成本，使药品价格制定的远高于其药品的内在价值。同时，单一的成本定价也助长了药企通过抬高成本转嫁成为价格而谋取更多的利润。药品集中招标的初衷是希望通过以竞价方式解决“药价虚高”的问题，实现药品采购过程的“阳光化”，纠正药品采购中的不正之风。在实施药品“购销零差率”之前医院销售药品时执行的是在政府招标的购进价基础上加成15%销售，在药品加成率固定的情况下，中标药品价格越低，医院药品经销利润则越少，因此，不难理解为何医院会选择高价药购进。同时，一些基本目录的常用廉价药，医药生产企业不愿意生产或供应断档脱销，或“改头换面”成为高价新药进入到招标目录中。

随着医改的进一步深入，公立医院药品零加成已经在全国多个地区展开。按照之前的规划，药品零加成之后医院收入减少的部分将主要由提高医院的服务性收入来弥补，剩下的20%分别由政府的财政补贴和医院自身削减成本来补充。但公立医院的服务性收入长期以来维持低价，短期内大幅提高仍有一定的难度，总体仍存在一定的缺口。公立医院长期以来不计成本的扩张引发医疗成本居高不下，快速降低成本的难度较大。为符合政策的要求及维持原发展态势，公立医院急需转嫁自身成本并弥补药品零加成所带来的收入下降。

using the differences in taxes and stealing or avoiding taxes.

By implementing the Two-invoice System in the purchase and sale of drugs, it has been expected to regulate and control the number of circulation of drugs from production, circulation of drugs to the terminals at hospitals so as to regulate the behaviors of purchase and sale of drugs, and to reduce and simplify the circulation links. In such way it is expected to eliminate the drug price markups, substantially reduce drug prices and serve the policy goal of the comprehensive medical care reform, while realizing the regulation and treatment of the pharmaceutical industry.

By implementing the Two-invoice System and reducing the circulation links of drugs, it is expected that on the one hand we could control the drug prices; on the other hand, we could promote the integration of the production and circulation industries of drugs, weed out the excessive small commercial companies and purify the circulation environment so as to facilitate the healthy growth of the pharmaceutical industry.

Looking back into the past, we learn that the drug prices were set by adding not more than 15% on the basis of the actual purchasing prices in 2006. As a result, the medical expenses increased instead of decrease. Prior to the full implementation of "the policy of purchasing drugs without adding profits", the pricing system featured the increase of prices on the basis of the prime costs prevailed in the purchase and sale of drugs in China; however, in the drug market which featured the serious information asymmetry, enterprises possessed all kinds of cost-related information such as R&D, production and management of drugs and occupied an absolute dominant position in the domain of information. On the contrary, the governmental regulatory organizations were lack of definite information of all kinds of costs of the drug production, thus being rendered in an inferior position in terms of information. In such circumstances, pharmaceutical enterprises would set the prices far above the intrinsic value of their drugs by means of setting false items of costs. At the same time, the singular cost pricing had encouraged pharmaceutical enterprises to obtain more profits by raising costs and increasing prices. The primary intention of the centralized procurement of drugs was to realize the sunshine purchase of drugs, solve the problem of "price markups" through the bidding, and curb or eliminate the bad practice in the procurement of drugs. Prior to the implementation of the policy of purchasing drugs without added profits in the purchase and sale of drugs, the drugs were purchased at the prices of adding 15% on the basis of the purchasing prices at the government tender. Under the circumstance that drug price addition rate was fixed, the lower the prices of the drugs winning the bid were, the less the distribution profits for the drugs for hospitals would be; therefore, it is not difficult for us to understand why the hospitals would select the high-priced drugs. Meanwhile, pharmaceutical manufacturers were unwilling to produce those common drugs at a low price which were included in the base directory, or failed the supply of such drugs, or such drugs would be converted into high-price new drugs through "changing faces" before being incorporated in the catalogue of tender.

As the medical care reform further deepened, the policy of drugs without price addition has been implemented in a couple of regions in China. In accordance with the previous planning, the income reduction of hospitals upon the adoption of such policy would be supplemented by increasing the service income of hospitals, while the residual 20% would be subsidized by the government and the reduction of costs by hospitals themselves. However, the service income of public hospitals have for

由此，“两票制”政策常伴随医药行业饱受争议的“二次议价”行为，两项政策常常形成合力，影响药品生产流通和使用全过程。

4. 财税政策

药品购销“两票制”并非孤立的医改政策，其全面实施带来的意义应与其他相关政策结合起来分析。“两票制”政策诞生于我国财税体制改革的背景之下，尤其是“金税工程”和全面实施的“营改增”财税政策。

过往医药生产和流通行业大面积采用违规“挂靠、走(过)票”方式运行。“营改增”实施后，传统的费用票据抵扣链条被斩断堵死，“底价包销”式营销格局被打破，采取“底价模式”运行的国内药品生产企业和少数外资合资企业面临财税管理全面调整。工业企业开票必须从“底价”转为正常票面价格开票，工业企业财税体系面对最大的变化是账面营业收入大幅增加，相应财税结构亦面临重大调整。同时，药品生产企业内部面临功能和架构改革、重组；产品销售模式和渠道面临重塑。为了解决“两票制”的实施给药企带来两方面的财税难题，药企须从业务源头开始重塑新的商业模式，用财务掩盖业务中的漏洞，用模式化解财务中的风险。

在“营改增 + 两票制”的体制下，如果工业企业选择高开发票，不仅会增加税收负担，而且还加大了销售费用向下游经销人员分摊的难度。大型商业公司可借势整合基层经销渠道（渠道优化），让生产企业可以选择部分低开的方式来降低成本，实现行业集中和产业链上下游双赢。“营改增”政策的实施，对于最上游的医药原材料供应商而言，各项费用严格计入税控系统，使其经营成本增加（扩展），势必相应提高原材料销售价格；下游最大终端医疗机构的压力则来自逐步实施药品“零加成”所减少的纯利。供应链上下游压力传导，将迫使中间医药流通企业微薄的利润空间进一步受到挤压。由此，医药流通企业面临市场的严酷考验。但同时，“营改增”的实施虽然对供应链上的各个环节造成了一定的影响，但它的实施，消除了生产服务业与生产企业之间的重复征税，从整体上降低了企业的税负水平。

a long time been maintained at a low level so that there would be some difficulty in the substantial increase of the service income in a short term, thus rendering a gap by and large. The public hospitals have for a long time kept expanding regardless of costs, which results in the medical costs' staying at a high level, making it difficult to rapidly reduce the costs. To meet the requirements of policies and maintain the original development trend, the public hospitals should urgently transfer their own costs and make up the decrease of income brought about by the zero addition in the drug pricing.

Hence, the implementation of the Two-invoice System has usually accompanied with the disputed behavior of "secondary price negotiation". The two polices often forms a kind of joint force which affects the whole process of the production, circulation and use of drugs.

4. Fiscal and taxation policies

The Two-invoice System in the purchase and sale of drugs is not an isolated medical care reform policy. The significance of the full implementation of it should be analyzed in combination with other relevant policies. The Two-invoice System was born in the background of the fiscal taxation system reform in China, especially the Golden Tax Project and the fiscal policies of Business Tax Replaced with Value-added Tax in the full implementation.

In the past, the pharmaceutical manufacturing and circulation industries operated by extensively adopting the illegal practices such as "the affiliation with an enterprise with relevant qualification, the business featuring the improper use of invoices issued by pharmaceutical enterprises and the business of intermediaries which engage in the business of drugs despite of their lack of relevant qualification". Upon the implementation of the Business Tax Replaced with Value-added Tax, the traditional chain wherein the bills for charges were deducted had been cut off and the marketing situation which featured "the exclusive sales at floor price" had been broken. For such, the domestic pharmaceutical manufacturers operating as per the "floor-price model" and a few foreign joint venture enterprises were faced with the across-the-board adjustment of financing and tax management. When issuing invoices, the industrial enterprises must issue invoices by shifting from "the floor price" to the normal par value, and the financial system of the industrial enterprises were faced with the biggest change: the substantial increase of par value of operating income and the significant adjustment for the corresponding financial and tax structure. At the same time, the pharmaceutical manufacturers were faced with the reform and recombination of functions and framework inside them; and the product sales models and channels should be reshaped. To solve the financial and tax problems brought about to the pharmaceutical enterprises due to the implementation of the Two-invoice System, the pharmaceutical enterprises should commence the reshaping of their commercial models from the sources of their business; namely, they should eliminate the loopholes in the business and solve the risks in the financial business by means of patterns.

In the system of the Business Tax Replaced with Value-added Tax + the Two-invoice System, if the industrial enterprises select the over-invoicing, they would not only add the tax burden, but increase the difficulty in apportioning the marketing expenses to sales personnel at the downstream. Large commercial companies can integrate the distribution channels or optimize the channels by taking advantage of the situation, enable industrial enterprises to reduce costs by writing invoice at a lower price in part, thus realizing the industrial concentration and the win-win goal at the downstream

5. 产业政策

《“十三五”深化医药卫生体制改革规划》颁布实施以来，医药卫生事业各项工作获得了重大进展和明显成效。作为医药卫生事业中重要的一环——医药产业的发展亦取得长足进步。医药工业总产值从启动第三轮医改之初2009年全行业的9000多亿元，快速增长至2016年年末近40 000亿元。行业快速发展一方面与整个国民社会发展水平相关；另一方面，全民医保体系建立之后，社会各方加大医疗卫生投入、行业发展逐渐从规模扩张外延式发展转型为内涵增长式发展，成为医药产业发展最强劲的动力源泉。

目前，我国药品研发由“仿制药为主、中西并重”向“跟踪仿制、局部创新、完全创新”转型；同时，医药行业供给侧改革提高了我国医药行业企业的创新能力。国家的政策改革从药品研发和生产环节改革入手，大力鼓励创新，扶持自主研发，鼓励开发具有突出临床价值、发展前景广阔的创新和仿制药品。具体而言，强调紧缺药品、大病防治、创新器械优先审批，在保证审批流程的严谨的前提下，提高效率。大力扶持创新产品上市。提升供给质量的同时拓广市场，走自主品牌的道路。短期内，仿制药品要对药品加紧筛查，从临床需求出发，综合考虑药品专利情况和市场潜力，完成药品规范化评价。完善自身运营状况的同时选择专业机构合作，发挥专业优势，开展药品研发工作。

of the industrial chain. For the suppliers of the raw materials of drugs at the farthest upstream, the implementation of the Business Tax Replaced with Value-added Tax means the incorporation of all kinds of expenses into the tax control system, thus causing the increase of their operating costs and certainly correspondingly enhancing the sales prices of the raw materials. At the same time, the largest terminal medical institutions at the downstream met the pressure from the decrease of net profits due to the implementation of the policy of the zero addition in the drug pricing. The pressure transfer of the supply chain at the upstream and downstream would force the intermediary drug circulation enterprises to further squeeze their meager profit margin; hence, the drug circulation enterprises were faced with the ordeal of the market. Meanwhile, despite the fact that the implementation of the Business Tax Replaced with Value-added Tax had to some degree affected the links in the supply chain, it had actually eliminated the repeated taxation between the production service industry and the manufacturing enterprises so as to reduce the enterprises' tax burden level on the whole.

5. Industrial policy

Since the promulgation and implementation of the *Plan of Deepening the Reform of the Medical and Health Sectors in the 13th Five-year Period*, significant progress and obvious effects had been made in all kinds of work in the medical and health career. As one of the important links, the pharmaceutical industry had also made great headway. The total output of the pharmaceutical industry rapidly increased from more than 900 billion yuan in 2009, the beginning of the launching of the 3rd-round medical care reform, to nearly 4 trillion yuan at the end of 2016. This rapid development was related to the whole national social development level on the one hand; upon the establishment of the universal medical insurance system, all relevant parties in the society had increased their investment in the medical treatment and public health sectors on the other hand. As a result, the industrial development had gradually shifted from the extended development featuring the scale expansion to the development featuring the connotative growth, thus becoming the most powerful source of power for the development of the pharmaceutical industry.

In the current drug R&D in China, a shift is made from "focused on generic drugs and paying equal attention to both Chinese and western drugs" to "tracing and imitating foreign drugs, making innovation in certain areas and adopting the comprehensive innovation". Meanwhile, the supply-side reform in the pharmaceutical industry has enhanced the innovative capability of pharmaceutical enterprises in China. In the policy reform in China, priority was given to the drug R&D and the production process, wherein innovation was greatly encouraged, independent R&D was supported and pharmaceutical enterprises were encouraged to develop innovative and generic drugs which feature the outstanding clinical value and a broad development prospect. Specifically speaking, the efficiency should be enhanced on the precondition that the approval with respect to the scarce drugs, the prevention and treatment of serious diseases and innovative and new medical equipment should be prioritized. Great support should be given to the launching of innovative products. We should expand the market while enhancing the quality of supply; and pharmaceutical enterprises are encouraged to build their own brands. In the short run, we should step up the screening of generic drugs; we should consider pharmaceutical patents and the market potential in a comprehensive manner from clinical demands so as to complete the standardized evaluation of drugs. We should improve our own operating

2017年2月21日，中国政府网发布《国务院关于印发“十三五”国家食品安全规划和“十三五”国家药品安全规划的通知》（以下简称《医药“十三五”规划》）。《医药“十三五”规划》中明确规定：医药卫生事业发展坚持政府主导与发挥市场机制作用相结合。在基本医疗卫生服务领域，坚持政府主导，落实政府责任，适当引入竞争机制。在非基本医疗卫生服务领域，发挥市场活力，加强规范引导，满足多样化、差异化、个性化健康需求；坚持推进供给侧结构性改革。实行政事分开、管办分开、医药分开、营利性和非营利性分开，优化供给侧治理能力和要素配置，提升服务效率和质量。对需求侧进行科学引导，合理划分政府、社会、个人责任，促进社会共治；坚持医疗、医保、医药联动改革。按照腾空间、调结构、保衔接的要求，统筹推进管理、价格、支付、薪酬等制度建设，提高政策衔接和系统集成能力。落实部门责任，解放思想、主动作为，以自我革命的精神推进改革，形成强大合力。坚持突出重点、试点示范、循序推进。理清改革内在逻辑，突出重要领域和关键环节，及时总结推广地方经验，发挥重点改革的突破性作用和试点的带动效应。把握好改革的力度和节奏，注重统筹兼顾，积极稳妥推进改革。

（1）深化药品供应领域改革

当前，人民生活水平不断提高，健康需求日益增长，但我国卫生资源总量不足、结构不合理、分布不均衡、供给主体相对单一、基层服务能力薄弱等问题仍比较突出，维护和促进人民健康的制度体系仍需不断完善。特别是随着医改进入攻坚期和深水区，深层次体制机制矛盾的制约作用日益凸显，利益格局调整更加复杂，改革的整体性、系统性和协同性明显增强，任务更为艰巨。同时，我国经济发展进入新常态，工业化、城镇化、人口老龄化进程加快，以及疾病谱变化、生态环境和生活方式变化、医药技术创新等，都对深化医改提出了更高要求。面对新的形势和挑战，需要在巩固前期改革成果、认真总结经验的基础上，进一步统一思想、坚定信念、增强定力，进一步加强组织领导、制度创新和重点突破，推动医改由打好基础转向提升质量、由形成框架转向制度建设、由单项突破转向系统集成和综合推进。

conditions, while selecting professional institutions for cooperation. The pharmaceutical enterprises should use their own professional advantages and conduct the drug R&D work.

On February 21, 2017, the Chinese government website released the *Notice of the State Council on the Issuance of the 13th Five-year National Food Safety Plan and the 13th Five-year National Drug Safety Plan* (short for "The 13th Five-year Plan of Pharmaceutical Industry"). The 13th Five-year Plan of Pharmaceutical Industry specifies that in the development of the drug and health career we should insist on the combination of the dominance by government and the mechanism role of the market. In the basic drug and health service domain, we should adhere to the dominance by government, carry out governmental responsibilities and properly introduce the competition mechanism. In the non-basic drug and health service domain, we should use the market vitality, strengthen the standardization and guidance and satisfy the demands of diversification, differentiation and personalized health; we should continue promoting the supply-side structure reform. We should adhere to the policy of separation of public service units from government, separation of management from operation, separation of clinic from pharmacy and separation of profit-seeking units from non-profit-seeking units; we should optimize the supply-side governance capability and the disposition of key elements, and enhance the service efficiency and quality. We should scientifically guide the demand-side and reasonably classify the responsibilities of the government, society and individuals and promote the social governance. We should insist on the reform with the interaction of medical area, medical insurance and pharmacy. We should in accordance with the requirements of making space, adjusting structure and ensuring connection push the construction of the systems of management, price, payment and remuneration in a coordinated manner and enhance the capability of the policy link-up and the system integration. We should implement the responsibilities of departments, free our minds and act initiatively. We should promote the reform with the spirit of self-revolution and thus form the powerful joint force. We should insist on highlighting key points, conducting demonstration on the site and pushing the reform in an orderly manner. We should make clear the internal logic of the reform, highlight the important domain and key links, timely summarize and promote local experiences, cause the role of breakthrough in the key reform into play and make use of the driving effect of experiment units. We should properly measure the strength and tempo of the reform, stress the overall planning and all-round consideration and positively and steadily push the reform.

(1) Deepen the reform of the supply domain of drugs

Currently, people's livelihood has constantly improved, with an increasing demand for health service; however, we have suffered from such headaches as insufficient total health resources, unreasonable structure, imbalanced distribution, comparative singularity in terms of the main bodies of supply and the weakness in the service capability so that we still have to keep improving the system of safeguarding and promoting people's health. In particular, as the medical care reform enters the critical period or the deep water area, the restrictive function caused by the in-depth institutional contradictions has become increasingly obvious; the adjustment of the benefit pattern has become more complicated; the integrality, systematicness and cooperativity of the reform has become evidently stronger; and the mission has become more difficult. At the same time, the economic development in China has entered the new normal period; the process of industrialization, urbanization and aging of population

通过市场倒逼和产业政策引导，推动企业提高创新和研发能力，促进做优做强，提高产业集中度，推动医药产业生产现代化和标准化，实现药品医疗器械质量达到或接近国际先进水平，打造中国标准和中国品牌。建立更加科学、高效的药品审评审批体系。加快推进仿制药质量和疗效一致性评价，鼓励创制新药，鼓励以临床价值为导向的药物创新。解决好低价药的供应问题。扶持低价药品生产，保障市场供应，保持药价基本稳定。建立健全短缺药品监测预警和分级应对机制，加快推进紧缺药品生产，支持建设小品种药物集中生产基地，继续开展用量小、临床必需、市场供应短缺药品的定点生产试点。完善儿童用药、卫生应急药品保障机制。对原料药市场供应不足的药品加强市场监测，鼓励提高生产能力。

（2）深化药品流通体制改革

加大药品、耗材流通行业结构调整力度，引导供应能力均衡配置，加快构建药品流通全国统一开放、竞争有序的市场格局，破除地方保护，形成现代流通新体系。推动药品流通企业兼并重组，整合药品经营企业仓储资源和运输资源，加快发展药品现代物流，鼓励区域药品配送城乡一体化。推动流通企业向智慧型医药服务商转型，建设和完善供应链集成系统，支持流通企业向供应链上下游延伸开展服务。应用流通大数据，拓展增值服务深度和广度，引导产业发展。鼓励绿色医药物流发展，发展第三方物流和冷链物流。

has accelerated; plus the changes to the spectrum of diseases, the ecological environment and lifestyle as well as the innovation of medical technologies; all of these have combined to raised high demands for the deepening of the medical care reform. In front of the new situation and challenges, we need to consolidate the reform achievements at the earlier stage and faithfully summarize the experiences, on the basis of which we should further unify our thinking, keep our faith, strengthen our willpower and further strengthen the organizational leadership, institutional innovation and key breakthroughs. In the pushing of the reform, we should shift from laying a good foundation to enhancement of quality, from forming of a framework to the institutional construction, and from the breakthrough in a single project to the system integration.

Under the pressure of the market in a reverse manner and the guidance of the industrial policies, we should push the enterprises to increase their capability of innovation and research and development, strive to be better and stronger, enhance the industrial concentration, promote the modernization and standardization of pharmaceutical manufacturing, promote the quality of domestic drugs and medical equipment to reach or near the international advanced level and create the Chinese standards and brands. We should build the drug evaluation and approval system which is more scientific and efficient. We should enhance the consistency evaluation on the quality and efficacy of generic drugs and encourage the development of new drugs and the drug innovation with the clinical value as the orientation. We should solve the problem of the supply of low-price drugs. We should support the production of them, guarantee the supply of them in the market and maintain the basic stability of drug prices. We should set up and improve the monitoring and early warning as well as the graded response mechanisms for drugs, speed up the production of scarce drugs and support the construction of the concentrated production bases of drugs featuring small varieties. We should continue conducting the production experiment at fixed places of drugs which feature small quantity in use, but are essential for clinical service and short of supply in the market. We should perfect the guarantee mechanism for drugs for children and the emergency drugs. We should strengthen the supervision on the drugs whose raw materials are in short supply in the market and encourage the relevant enterprises to raise their production capability.

(2) Deepen the reform of the drug circulation system

We should further adjust the circulation industry structure of drugs and medical consumables, guide the balanced allocation of the supply ability, step up the construction of the market pattern of drug circulation in China which features unity, openness and orderly competition, eliminate the local protection and form the modern circulation system. We should promote the M&A and recombination of drug circulation enterprises, integrate the warehousing and transportation resources of drug operating enterprises, speed up the modern drug logistics and encourage the urban-rural integration of drugs at the regional level. We should push circulation enterprises to transform themselves into intelligent pharmaceutical service companies, construct and perfect the supply chain integrated system and support circulation enterprises to extend their service to the upstream and downstream of the supply chain. We should make use of the circulation big data, expand the depth and breadth of the value-added services and guide the industrial development. We should encourage the development of the green medical logistics industry and develop the third-party logistics and the cold-chain logistics.

（3）完善国家药物政策体系

健全管理体制，建立国家药物政策协调机制。推动医药分开，采取综合措施切断医院和医务人员与药品、耗材间的利益链。医疗机构应按照药品通用名开具处方，并主动向患者提供，不得限制处方外流。探索医院门诊患者多渠道购药模式，患者可凭处方到零售药店购药。推动企业充分竞争和兼并重组，提高市场集中度，实现规模化、集约化和现代化经营。调整市场格局，使零售药店逐步成为向患者售药和提供药学服务的重要渠道。进一步完善药品价格形成机制，强化价格、医保、采购等政策的衔接，坚持分类管理，实行不同的价格管理方式，逐步建立符合我国药品市场特点的药价管理体系。建立健全医保药品支付标准，结合仿制药质量和疗效一致性评价工作，逐步按通用名制定药品支付标准。完善国家医药储备体系，在应急保障的基础上，完善常态短缺药品储备。完善中药政策，加强中药材质量管理，鼓励中药饮片、民族药的临床应用。探索建立医院总药师制度，完善医疗机构和零售药店药师管理制度，结合医疗服务价格改革，体现药事服务价值。建立药物临床综合评价体系和儿童用药临床综合评价机制，提高合理用药水平。

（4）深化医药卫生领域“放管服”改革

按照简政放权、放管结合、优化服务的要求，推进医药卫生领域行政审批制度改革。对确需保留的行政审批事项，建立清单制度并向社会公示。转变监管理念，创新监管机制和监管方式，更加注重加强事中事后监管，提升监管效能。优化政府服务，提高服务水平。促进医疗卫生机构转变服务模式，改善服务质量。

(3) Improve the national pharmaceutical policy system

We should perfect the management system and set up the national pharmaceutical policy coordination mechanism. We should promote the separation of clinic from pharmacy and adopt comprehensive measures to cut off the profit chain between hospitals and medical personnel in respect of drugs and medical consumables. The medical institutions should prescribe as per the approved names of drugs and initiatively provide them to patients, without preventing the prescriptions from being exposed. We should explore the multiple-channel procurement model for outpatients at hospitals and the patients can purchase drugs at drugstores with the prescriptions. We should push the full competition and M&A and recombination among enterprises, enhance the market concentration, and realize the scaled, concentrated and modern operation. We should adjust the market pattern so as to enable drugstores to gradually become the important channels of selling drugs to patients and providing medical services. We should further perfect the pricing mechanism of drugs and strengthen the connection between the policies of price, medical insurance and procurement. We should insist on the systematic management and adopt the different price management methods, thus gradually forming the drug price management system which coincides with the characteristics of the pharmaceutical market in China. We should perfect the payment standard for drugs within the medical insurance system. We should in combination with the consistence evaluation of the quality and efficacy of generic drugs gradually formulate the payment standards for the drugs as per the approved names thereof. We should perfect the national pharmaceutical storage system and on the basis of the emergency and security perfect the storage of the normally scarce drugs. We should perfect the policies of traditional Chinese drugs, strengthen the quality management of traditional Chinese medicinal materials and encourage the clinical application of Chinese herbal pieces and ethnic drugs. We should explore the system of general pharmacists at hospitals, perfect the pharmacist management system at medical institutions and drugstores and in combination with the medical service price reform reflect the value of pharmaceutical service. We should establish the comprehensive evaluation system for the clinical use of drugs and the comprehensive evaluation mechanism for the clinical use of drugs for children and enhance the rational drug use level.

(4) Deepen the reform of "streamlining administration and delegating power to lower levels, combining the easing of restrictions and the management, and optimizing services"

In accordance with the requirements of "streamlining administration and delegating power to lower levels, combining the easing of restrictions and the management, and optimizing services", we should push the reform of the administrative approval system in the medical and health domain. For the affairs concerning the government review and approval which needs to be preserved, we should establish the system of lists and make them known to the public. We should change the concept of supervision, create new supervision mechanism and methods, pay more attention to the supervision in the process of and after the events and enhance the supervisory efficiency. We should optimize the governmental service and increase the service level. We should promote the medical and health institutions to change their service models and improve their service quality.

（5）引导规范第三方评价和行业自律

完善相关政策制度，鼓励符合条件的第三方积极开展或参与评价标准的咨询、技术支持、考核评价等工作，推动医疗机构考核评价由政府主导逐步向独立第三方评价转变。充分发挥行业协会学会、高等院校、科研院所等的作用，积极培育第三方评价机构。强化行业自律，推动行业组织建立健全行业管理规范和准则，规范成员行为。引导和规范医疗机构建立内审制度，加强自我管理和自查自纠，提高医疗服务质量，保障医疗安全。加强全国医疗卫生行业监管信息管理，为医疗机构开展业务及提升服务质量、服务效率、满意度等提供有效监控依据。

（6）在政府指导下发挥市场机制在药品生产流通领域对资源配置的基础性作用

2009 年以来推行的医药卫生体制改革体系认为，我国医药领域发展的首要条件是建立严格规范的综合监管制度。通过健全医药卫生法律体系，加快转变政府职能，完善与医药卫生事业发展相适应的监管模式，提高综合监管效率和水平，推进监管法制化和规范化，建立健全职责明确、分工协作、运行规范、科学有效的综合监管长效机制。由于市场存在失灵状况，经济的运行不能完全依靠市场机制的自发作用，客观上需要政府的干预和调控，即通过发挥政府在资源配置中的作用来弥补市场缺陷，克服市场失灵，促进社会经济的协调运行。政府职能部门要提高监管和服务能力，创造良好的市场环境。从政策上鼓励新特药的研发，限制不同类型药品之间的恶性竞争，促使制药企业从营销竞争转向技术创新竞争，建立公平合理的竞争环境。针对大型企业因过分追求利益而选择性地采购药品的行为，要及时监管，有效干预。

(5) Guide and regulate the third-party comments and the self-regulation of the industry

We should perfect the relevant policies and systems, encourage the qualified third-party to positively conduct or participate in such work as consulting of the assessment criteria, technological support and examination and evaluation, push the examination and evaluation of medical institutions to shift gradually from the governmental dominance to the independent third-party evaluation. We should fully play the roles of the industrial associations, higher learning institutions and scientific research institutions, etc. and positively cultivate the third-party evaluation institutions. We should strengthen the self-regulation of the industry, push the industrial organizations to establish and perfect the management standards and principles of the whole industry and regulate the behaviors of the members of the industry. We should guide and regulate medical institutions to establish the internal auditing system, strengthen the self-management and self-examination and rectification system, enhance the medical service quality and guarantee the medical safety. We should strengthen the industrial supervision and information management of the medical and health sectors in the whole country and provide the effective supervisory evidence for the medical institutions in their conducting of business and enhancement of service quality and efficiency as well as the satisfaction of consumers, among others.

(6) We should under the guidance of the government play the fundamental role of the market mechanism in the pharmaceutical production and circulation domain in terms of resources allocation

The medical and health system reform which was launched in 2009 showed that the primary condition of the development in the pharmaceutical industry in China was to establish the strict and standard comprehensive supervisory system. We should through perfecting the medical and health legal system step up the shift of the governmental functions, perfect the supervisory model which adapts to the development of the medical and health career, enhance the comprehensive supervision efficiency and level, push the legislation and standardization of the supervision and establish the comprehensive and long-term mechanism which features clear duties, coordination and distribution of responsibilities, regulated operation and scientific and effective functioning. Given the failure of the market, the operation of the economy cannot fully rely on the spontaneous role of the market mechanism. Objectively the intervention and adjustment of the government is needed; namely, we should play the role of the government in the allocation of resources to make up for the market defects, overcome the market failure and promote the coordinated operation of the social economy. The functional departments of the government should enhance the supervisory and service capabilities and create an excellent market environment. We should based on the policies encourage the enterprises to research and develop new and special drugs, restrict the vicious competition between drugs of different types, facilitate the pharmaceutical manufacturers to shift from the marketing competition to the technological innovation competition and establish the fair and reasonable competition environment. We should timely supervise the behaviors of the large enterprises which desire to selectively purchase drugs for excessive benefits and effectively intervene in such behaviors.

（二）实施药品购销“两票制”政策的产业环境和技术条件

实施药品购销“两票制”政策的产业环境和技术条件如图 5 所示。

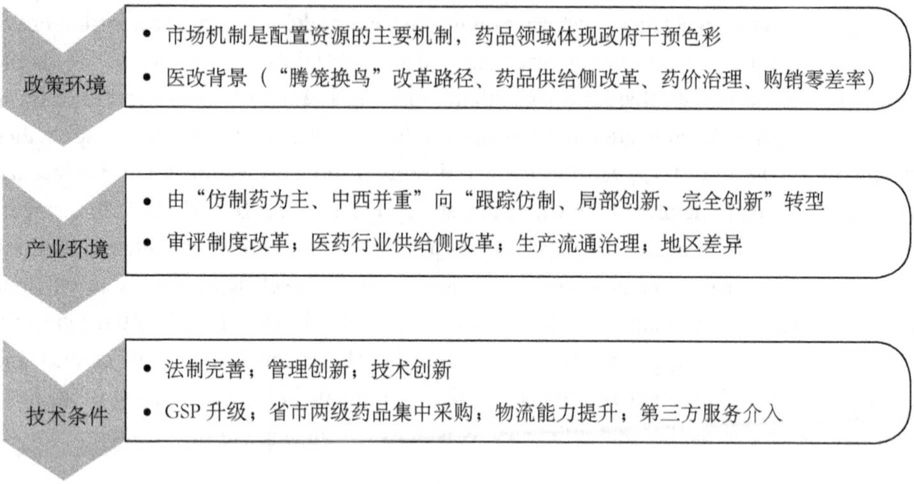

图 5　实施药品购销“两票制”政策的产业环境和技术条件

(II) The industrial environment and technological conditions of the implementation of the Two-invoice System in the purchase and sale of drugs

The industrial environment and technological conditions of the implementation of the Two-invoice System in the purchase and sale of drugs are shown in Figure 5.

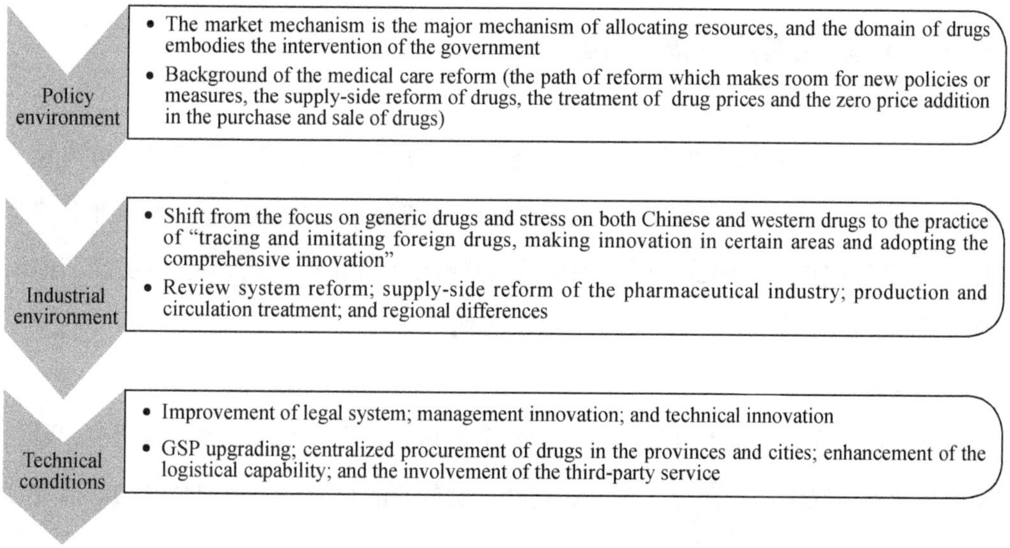

Figure 5 The industrial environment and technological conditions of the implementation of the Two-invoice System in the purchase and sale of drugs

六、“两票制”核心政策解析

（一）药品购销“两票制”的具体内容

1. 基本原则

“两票制”是指药品生产企业到流通企业开一次发票，流通企业到医疗机构开一次发票。公立医疗机构药品采购中要逐步实行“两票制”，鼓励其他医疗机构推行“两票制”。综合医改试点省和公立医院改革试点城市要率先推行“两票制”，鼓励其他地区执行“两票制”，争取到 2018 年在全国全面推开。

2. 例外情况

为应对自然灾害、重大疫情、重大突发事件和患者急（抢）救等特殊情况，紧急采购药品或国家医药储备药品，可特殊处理；麻醉药品和第一类精神药品的流通经营仍按国家现行规定执行。

限定为乡镇卫生院或村级医疗卫生机构的偏远基层可增加一票；制药企业销售给自有商业公司可不视为一票；医药流通企业向下属子公司销售可不视为一票；医药流通企业向偏远基层医疗机构销售可视为允许的第三票。

3. 药品购销票据管理规定

严格执行药品购销管理规定：集中采购机制编制采购文件时，要将执行“两票制”作为必备条件；对于招标采购的药品，要验明药品生产企业的资质，由药品生产企业直接投标；直接参与药品集中采购的生产企业和配送企业要在标书中做出执行“两票制”的承诺，否则投标无效；实行其他采购方式采购药品，也必须在采购合同中明确“两票制”的有关要求。

对于药品生产企业，应当按照发票管理有关规定开具增值税专用发票或者增值税普通发票，项目要填写齐全。所销售药品还应当按照《药品经营质量管理规范》（药品 GSP）要求附符合规定的随货同行单，发票（及清单）的购、销方名称应当与随货同行单、付款流向、金额一致。

VI. Analysis of the core policies of the Two-invoice System

(I) The concrete contents of the Two-invoice System in the purchase and sale of drugs

1. Basic principles

The Two-invoice System means that one invoice is issued to cover the process from the pharmaceutical manufacturers to the circulation enterprises, and the other invoice to cover the process from the circulation enterprises to the medical institutions. The Two-invoice System should be gradually implemented in the procurement of drugs for public medical institutions and other medical institutions should be encouraged to adopt the same. The provinces selected for the experiment of the medical care reform and the cities selected as the experiment units of the reform of public hospitals should take the lead in the implementation of the Two-invoice System, and other regions should be encouraged to adopt the same, thus striving to fully launch the same across the country in 2018.

2. Exceptions

To cope with natural disasters, major epidemics, significant incidents and first aid or rescue of patients, etc., special treatment can be given to the urgent procurement of drugs or storage of drugs of the State. The circulation and operation of narcotic drugs and psychotrophic substances Ⅰ should be handled as per the current provisions of the State.

The health clinics in towns and townships or the village-level medical and health organizations which are remotely located can be granted another invoice, and the sales from the pharmaceutical manufacturers to their own commercial companies may not be regarded as one invoice; the sales from the drug circulation enterprises to their subsidiaries may not be regarded as one invoice; and the sales from the drug circulation enterprises to the remote grassroots medical institutions can be allowed the third invoice.

3. Administrative regulations on bills of the drug procurement and sales

We should strictly implement the provisions of the drug procurement and sales management. When preparing the procurement and sales documents for the centralized procurement of drugs, we should take the Two-invoice System as an essential condition. For the drugs to be purchased through tendering, we should verify the qualification of the pharmaceutical manufacturers, which should directly participate in the tendering. The manufacturing enterprises and delivery enterprises which directly participate in the centralized procurement of drugs should make a promise of implementing the Two-invoice System in the biding documents; otherwise the bidding will be deemed as null and void. Where other purchase methods are adopted for the procurement of drugs, the relevant requirements of the Two-invoice System shall be specified in the purchase contracts.

The pharmaceutical manufacturers should issue the VAT special invoices or the VAT regular invoices as per the relevant provisions of the invoice management and the items shall be filled in full. All drugs to be sold shall be accompanied with the invoices in accordance with the requirements of the *Good Supply Practice*; the names of the purchasers and sellers on the invoices or lists shall be consistent with those on the bills accompanied with the goods; the direction of the payment shall be consistent; and the amounts shall be of the same.

对于药品流通企业，购进药品应主动向药品生产企业索要发票，发票必须由药品生产企业开具。到货验收时，应验明发票、供货方随货同行单与实际购进药品的品种、规格、数量等，核对一致并建立购进药品验收记录，做到票、货、账相符。对发票和随货同行单不符合国家有关规定要求，或者发票、随货同行单和购进药品之间内容不相符的，不得验收入库。药品购销中发生的发票及相关票据，应当按照有关规定保存。

公立医疗机构在药品验收入库时，必须验明票、货、账三者一致方可入库、使用，不仅要向配送药品的流通企业索要、验证发票，还应当要求流通企业出具加盖印章的由生产企业提供的进货发票复印件，两张发票的药品流通企业名称、药品批号等相关内容互相印证，且作为公立医疗机构支付药品货款凭证，纳入财务档案管理。每个药品品种的进货发票复印件至少提供一次。鼓励有条件的地区使用电子发票，通过信息化手段验证“两票制”。

对于偏远、交通不便的乡、村药品供应：允许在“两票制”基础上再开一次药品购销发票，但仅限于特别偏远、交通不便的乡（镇）和村级基层医疗卫生机构。对特殊药品及特殊情况下药品的采购：为应对自然灾害、重大疫情、重大突发事件和患者急（抢）救等特殊情况，紧急采购药品或国家医药储备药品，可实行特殊处理；对于麻醉药品和第一类精神药品的流通经营，仍按国家现行规定执行。

4. 监管

卫生部门对于索票（证）不严、“两票制”落实不到位，拖欠贷款，有令不行的医疗机构要通报批评，直到追究相关人员责任；药监部门：企业实施“两票制”情况纳入检查范围；税务部门：加强发票管理，依法加大对偷逃税行为的监管力度。推动药品集中采购平台（公共资源交易平台）、药品追溯体系和诚信体系建设平台等互联互通、数据共享，实现违法线索互联、监管标准互通、处理结果互认。

（二）“两票制”政策对各行政相关部门的要求

（1）各省（区、市）药品集中采购机构要加强药品集中采购工作监督管理，对不按规定执行“两票制”要求的药品生产企业、流通企业，取消投标、中标和配送资格，并列入药品采购不良记录。

The drug circulation enterprises shall demand invoices from the pharmaceutical manufacturers and the invoices shall be issued by the pharmaceutical manufacturers. At the time of inspection of incoming goods, the invoices, the bills accompanying the goods by the suppliers, as well as the varieties, specifications and quantity of the drugs actually purchased shall be verified. After the consistence is proved, the inspection records of the purchased drugs shall be made, thus ensuring the coincidence between the invoices, goods and accounts. Where the invoices and the bills accompanying the goods fail to meet the relevant provisions and requirements of the State, or the invoices and the bills accompanying the goods are inconsistent with the contents of the drugs purchased, they shall be kept as per relevant provisions.

When the public medical institutions inspect the drugs, they must verify the consistence between the invoices, goods and accounts before the drugs' being put into the warehouse and used. They shall not only demand and verify invoices from the circulation enterprises which distribute such drugs, but require them to submit the duplicates of the invoices for the purchased drugs as provided by the manufacturing enterprises and sealed with the company stamp of the circulation enterprises. The names of the drug circulation enterprises and the lot numbers of the drugs, among others, on the two invoices shall be mutually corroborated; and as the vouchers for the public medical institutions to pay the drugs, they shall be incorporated into the financial file management. The duplicates of the invoices for each kind of purchased goods shall be provided at least once. The areas with sufficient conditions are encouraged to use electronic invoices and verify the Two-invoice System through the information tools.

As for the supply of drugs for the townships and villages which are remotely located and inconveniently accessible, another invoice for the purchase and sale of drugs can be issued on the basis of the Two-invoice System, but such policy is only applicable for grassroots medical and health institutions at the towns and townships and villages which are remotely located and inconveniently accessible. For the procurement of special drugs and under the special circumstances, such as natural disasters, major epidemics, significant incidents and first aid and rescue of patients, special treatments can be given to the urgent procurement of drugs or the storage of drugs by the State. For the narcotic drugs and psychotrophic substances Ⅰ, the current provisions of the State shall be complied with.

4. Supervision

A notice of criticism will be circulated for the medical institutions which are not strict with invoices or vouchers, fail to implement the Two-invoice System, default in payment for goods and do not take relevant instructions, till the relevant personnel are investigated and claimed against their corresponding responsibilities. The implementation of the Two-invoice System by the enterprises shall be incorporated into the scope of inspection. The relevant department should strengthen the invoice management and intensify the crackdown upon the tax evasion. We should facilitate the connectivity and data sharing of the centralized drug procurement platform (the public resources transaction platform), the drug traceability system and the credit system construction platform so as to share the clues of violations and supervision standards, as well as the mutual recognition of the results of handling.

(II) Requirements of the policies of the Two-invoice System on the relevant administrative departments

(1) The agencies in charge of the centralized procurement of drugs in all provinces (autonomous regions and municipalities) shall tighten the supervision and administration of the centralized

(2)卫生计生、中医药行政部门要加强对公立医疗机构执行“两票制”的监督检查，对索票(证)不严、“两票制”落实不到位、拖欠货款、有令不行的医疗机构要通报批评，直到追究相关人员责任。

(3) 食品药品监督管理部门对药品生产、流通企业进行监督检查时，除检查企业落实《药品流通监督管理办法》和《药品经营质量管理规范》等有关规定外，还应当将企业实施“两票制”情况纳入检查范围。对企业违反“两票制”要求的情况，食品药品监管部门应当及时通报所在省份药品集中采购机构。涉嫌犯罪的，依法移送公安机关。税务部门要加强对药品生产、流通企业和医疗机构的发票管理，依法加大对偷逃税行为的稽查力度。

(4) 各相关部门要充分利用信息化手段，加强“两票制”执行情况的监督检查，建立健全跨部门、跨区域监管联动响应和协作机制，推动药品集中采购平台（公共资源交易平台）、药品追溯体系和诚信体系建设平台等互联互通、数据共享，实现违法线索互联、监管标准互通、处理结果互认。推进和加强信息公开、公示，广泛接受社会监督。国家相关部门将适时组织开展“两票制”落实情况的专项监督检查。

(5) 拓展新领域发展新业态。大力推动“互联网 + 医药”，发展智慧医疗产品。开发应用具备云服务和人工智能功能的移动医疗产品、可穿戴设备，各种类型的基于移动互联网的健康管理软件，可实现远程监护、咨询的远程医疗系统。加强对健康医疗大数据的开发和利用，发展电子健康档案、电子病历、电子处方等数据库，实现数据资源互联互通和共享，指导疾病诊治、药物评价和新药开发，发展基于大数据的医疗决策支持系统。推动生产性服务业和服务型制造发展。大力发展合同生产、合同研发、医药电子商务、生物技术服务、医疗器械第三方维护保养等新型生产性服务业，促进分工进一步专业化，提高效率和降低成本。

procurement of drugs, and the pharmaceutical manufacturers and distribution enterprises that fail to implement the Two-invoice System are disqualified from bidding, award of a bid and delivery of drugs and are listed in the register of bad conduct for drug procurement.

(2) Health and family planning departments and Chinese medicine administrative departments shall step up supervision and inspection of the implementation of the Two-invoice System in public medical institutions, and circulate a notice of criticism for medical institutions that do not demand the invoice (proof), fail to fully implement Two-invoice System, fall into arrears with payment of goods, and do not observe the orders, until the relevant personnel are held accountable.

(3) In addition to examining the implementation of *Provisions for Supervision of Drug Distribution* and *Good Supply Practice for Pharmaceutical Products* by enterprises, the food and drug supervision and administration departments shall also incorporate the implementation of Two-invoice System into the inspection scope when conducting supervision and inspection on pharmaceutical production and circulation enterprises. If an enterprise violates the Two-invoice System, the food and drug regulatory authority shall notify the agencies in charge of the centralized procurement of drugs in its province in a timely manner. An enterprise suspected of being involved in a crime shall be transferred to public security organs according to the law. Tax departments shall step up the management of invoices for drug production and distribution enterprises and medical institutions and step up the inspection of tax evasion in accordance with the law.

(4) All relevant departments shall make full use of the information technology to tighten the supervision and inspection of the implementation of the Two-invoice System, establish a sound inter-departmental and cross-regional regulatory linkage response and coordination mechanism, and promote the interconnectivity and date sharing among such platforms as centralized purchasing platform of drugs (public resources trading platform), drug traceability system and credit system construction platform, so as to achieve interconnection of clues of crime, interconnectivity of regulatory standards, and mutual recognition of the results. The departments concerned shall promote and strengthen information disclosure and publicity, and accept social supervision. Relevant state departments will organize the special supervision and inspection on the implementation of the Two-invoice System in due time.

(5) Expand new areas and develop new types of business. We shall promote the "Internet + medicine", and develop smart medical products. Efforts should be made to develop and use mobile medical products and wearable devices with cloud services and artificial intelligence capabilities, various types of mobile Internet-based health management software, and telemedicine systems for remote monitoring and counseling. We shall strengthen the development and utilization of big data for health and medical services, develop databases such as electronic health records, electronic medical records and electronic prescriptions, realize the interconnection and sharing of data resources, guide disease diagnosis and treatment, drug evaluation and new drug development, and develop medical decision-making support system based on big data. We shall promote the development of producer services and service-oriented manufacturing. We will vigorously develop new productive service industries such as contract manufacturing, contract research and development, pharmaceutical e-commerce, biotechnology services and third-party medical equipment maintenance, with a view to promoting specialization in division of labor, increasing efficiency and curtailing costs.

(6) 优化产业组织结构。推进行业重组整合。通过提高注册、质量、节能、环保、安全生产等标准，严格市场准入，形成市场倒逼机制，促进企业重组和落后企业退出。支持企业强强联合，培育具有国际竞争力的大型企业。推动大型医药企业整合中小型创新创业企业，促进新产品、新技术和已有产能对接。实施上市许可持有人制度试点，发展专业化委托生产业务，着力化解产能过剩。培育支持中小企业上市，促使企业规范公司治理结构，转换经营机制。鼓励社会资本发展并购基金，拓宽企业兼并重组融资渠道。

(7) 引导产业集聚发展。根据行业发展需要，结合各地资源禀赋和环境承载能力，科学规划产业集聚区。落实京津冀协同发展、长江经济带战略，引导产业跨区域资源整合。加强产业集聚区专业化基础设施、服务平台和人力资源条件建设，研究制定符合行业特点的专项支持政策，增强园区承载能力和服务能力，优化发展空间，提升发展水平。

(8) 增强产业创新能力。完善政产学研用协同创新体系。发挥政府的引导和推动作用，营造激励创新的政策环境。强化企业技术创新主体地位，发挥骨干企业整合科技资源的作用，扶持掌握关键技术的研发型小企业发展。推动企业加强与高校、科研院所和医疗机构技术协作，建立符合新药研发特点的投入、收益、风险分担机制，加速研发成果产业化。调动医疗机构在医药创新上的积极性，提高新药临床研究水平，促进科技成果转化和应用。推动创新升级。引导企业提高创新质量，培育重大产品，满足重要需求，解决重点问题，提升产业化技术水平。推动化学药研发从仿制为主向自主创新为主转移。

（三）药品购销“两票制”的政策目标

多份相关文件均指出，围绕公立医院改革目标，通过在医改先行地区试点、随后在全国范围推行公立医院药品集中采购的药品购销“两票制”，期望达到如下政策目标。

(6) Optimize the industrial structure. We shall promote industry restructuring and integration. By improving standards in registration, quality, energy conservation, environmental protection and safe production, we shall strictly enforce market access rules, use the market as a check, and promote the reorganization of enterprises and the exit of backward enterprises. We shall support the alliance of powerful enterprises to foster large-scale enterprises with international competitiveness; promote large pharmaceutical companies to integrate small and medium-sized innovative start-ups and promote coordination between new products and new technologies with existing production capacity; and implement the pilot scheme for marketing authorization holder system, develop specialized commissioned production operations and resolve overcapacity. Efforts shall be made to nurture and support the listing of SMEs, encourage enterprises to standardize their corporate governance structure and transform their mechanism for operations; and encourage the social capital to develop the M&A funds and broaden the financing channels for corporate mergers and acquisitions and restructuring.

(7) Guide the development of industrial agglomeration. According to the needs of the development of the industry, combined with resources and environmental carrying capacity of the local areas, we shall plan efficient industrial agglomerations. Efforts are made to implement the strategies of coordinated development of Beijing-Tianjin-Hebei, and the Yangtze River Economic Belt, and guide the industry cross-regional integration of resources. We will strengthen the construction of specialized infrastructure, service platforms and human resources conditions in industrial clusters, study and formulate special support policies in line with the characteristics of the industry, enhance the carrying capacity and service capacity of parks, optimize the space for development and upgrade the level of development.

(8) Enhance industrial innovation ability. We shall improve the collaborative innovation system of government, enterprises, universities, science institutes, and users; give play to the guidance and promotion role of the government and create a policy environment that encourages innovation; strengthen the principal position of technological innovation in enterprises, give play to the role of backbone enterprises in integrating science and technology resources, and support the development of small-sized R&D enterprises that master the key technologies. We will promote enterprises to cement cooperation with universities, research institutes and medical institutions regarding technology, establish investment, income and risk sharing mechanism in line with the characteristics of new drug research and development, and accelerate the commercialization of research and development achievements. Efforts are made to mobilize the enthusiasm of medical institutions in medical & pharmaceutical innovation, improve the clinical research of new drugs, promote the transformation and application of scientific and technological achievements, and spur innovation and upgrading. We shall guide enterprises to improve the quality of innovation, nurture major products, meet important needs, solve key issues and enhance the application of technology in product. We will shift the focus of chemical drugs from imitation to independent innovation.

(III) Policy objectives of the Two-invoice System in the purchase and sale of drugs

Relevant documents point out that the following policy objectives are expected to be achieved through the pilot project of “Two-invoice System for pharmaceutical procurement and sale” for

一是减少药品流通环节，规范流通秩序，提高流通效率，降低药品虚高价格。目前我国医药行业药品流通主要采用的还是“多票制”的开票模式，“多票制”的药品流通模式中间涉及多个环节，会经历多个代理商的多次开票。在这种流通模式下，各级代理商为了经济利益最大化，将会逐级抬高价格，到医疗机构终端必然会造成药价虚高。而“两票制”的意义就是减少药品流通环节，最大限度降低药品流通成本，降低药品价格。

二是加强药品监管，实现药品质量、价格可追溯，保障群众用药安全。在“多票制”环境下，流通环节过多，不稳定的运输条件和储存设施都会对药品的质量产生一定的威胁。并且在多环节的流通过程中，可能有假冒伪劣药品混入，给药品质量带来安全隐患。通过实施药品购销“两票制”，有利于实现对上述不规范现象的行业治理。

三是净化流通环境，治理药品流通领域乱象，依法打击非法挂靠、商业贿赂、偷逃税款等违法行为。“两票制”下，药品流通环节的缩减，更有利于加强对偷逃税款、商业贿赂等一系列灰色空间的监管。

四是助力深化药品领域改革，助推药品企业转型升级、做大做强，提高行业集中度，促进医药产业健康发展。我国药品流通企业规模较小，远低于国外企业规模，整个药品流通体系呈现多头、分散、缺乏比较集中的销售渠道。而在集中配送模式下，不符合药品经营许可规定的非法流通企业及一些通过过票走票而获取非法盈利的中小型企业将逐渐被淘汰，从而进一步增强市场集中度。

（四）在“两票制”体系下，政策细节及对各方的定义

1.“两票制”政策对于生产企业的认定

（1）国家版“两票制”文件所认可的几种情形

①药品生产企业或科工贸一体化的集团型企业设立的仅销售本企业（集团）药品的全资或控股商业公司（全国仅限一家商业公司）。

②境外药品国内总代理（全国仅限一家国内总代理）。

（2）地方版“两票制”政策对视同于生产企业的认定情形

①药品总经销权的境外授权、境内转授权。例如，默克雪兰诺公司在境外授权施贵宝公司在中国生产和销售二甲双胍缓释片，后者将二甲双胍缓释片的国内经销权归

the centralized procurement of drugs in public hospitals in the pilot areas for medical reform, and subsequent the whole country.

First, reduce circulation links of drug, standardize the circulation order, improve circulation efficiency, and lower the extortionate prices of medicines. At present, the drug circulation in China mainly adopts the invoicing mode of "Multiple-invoice System". The drug circulation mode of "Multiple-invoice System" involves multiple links and concerns multiple invoicing by multiple agents. In this mode of circulation, agents at all levels, in order to maximize economic benefits, will raise the price step by step, resulting in extortionate prices of medicines at the medical institutions. The idea of the Two-invoice System is to reduce the drug circulation, minimize the cost of drug distribution and curtail the price of medicines.

Second, strengthen drug regulation, achieve drug quality, traceability of price, and ensure the safe use of drugs for the public. In the "Multiple-invoice System", excessive circulation, unstable shipping conditions and storage facilities pose a threat to the quality of medicines. In the process of circulation of medicines, fake and shoddy drugs may enter the circulation process, bringing potential safety hazard to the quality of medicines. The implementation of Two-invoice System for pharmaceutical purchase and sale is conducive to the regulation of the aforesaid irregularities in the pharmaceutical industry.

Third, purify the circulation environment, cure the chaos in the field of drug circulation, and crack down on illegal acts such as illegal affiliation, commercial bribery and tax evasion in accordance with the law. Under the Two-invoice System, the shorter medicine circulation process contributes to strengthening the regulation of gray spaces such as tax evasion and commercial bribery.

Fourth, help deepen the reform in the pharmaceutical sector, boost the transformation and upgrading of pharmaceutical enterprises and help them become bigger and stronger, increase industry concentration and promote the healthy development of the pharmaceutical industry. China's pharmaceutical distribution enterprises are far smaller than foreign enterprises, and the entire pharmaceutical distribution system is scattered, without a centralized sales channel. In the centralized distribution mode, however, the illegal circulation enterprises that do not meet the requirements of the drug supply certificate and small and medium-size unlicensed enterprises that obtain illegal profits through the practice of engaging in drug supply activities using others' permit will be gradually eliminated, thereby enhancing market concentration.

(IV) Policy details and definitions for all parties under the Two-invoice System

1. Identification of manufacturing enterprises under the Two-invoice System policy

(1) Situations recognized by the state-level document on the Two-invoice System

① Wholly-owned or controlled commercial companies (only one commercial company in the country) established by drug manufacturing enterprises or group-type enterprises integrating R&D, production and marketing for the purpose of selling only the medicines of the enterprise (group).

②Domestic general agent of foreign drugs (only one domestic general agent in the country).

(2) Situations under which production enterprises are recognized under local versions of the Two-invoice System policy

① The overseas authorization and domestic sublicensing right of general agency of drugs. For

还给默克雪兰诺在中国的分支机构进行销售。

②联合开发，生产、经销权分离。例如，礼来公司与和黄制药联合开发小分子抗肿瘤药呋喹替尼，和黄制药持有药品批准文号，而将国内经销权授予礼来公司。

③ MAH 持证人授权。

④境外生产，进口总代理。

⑤境内生产，国内总代理。

“两票制”政策执行初期，重庆、云南、广西、海南四地地方版“两票制”政策（含意见稿）曾认可国内药品生产企业设置的唯一国内总代理商业企业可以视同于药品生产企业。至 2017 年 11 月，重庆、云南两地陆续放弃了相关条款，保持与国家版方案一致。

对于是否认可国内企业境内唯一总代理作为药品生产企业，各地“两票制”政策甚至包括相关行业各方，均存在着较大的争议。

包括部分地方官员和学者在内的支持方认为，在全国实施“两票制”购销政策的背景下，应给予国内企业和外资企业同样的市场待遇，既然允许外资企业的唯一进口商及境外生产境内销售唯一总代理商视同为生产企业，则亦同样应给予国内企业相关待遇，以符合社会经济发展的宏观方向。同时，在《药品管理法》进行修订后，国内药品生产行业普遍推行生产许可持证人制度（MAH），未来，药品的生产和销售相分离将成为普遍现象，这也是国际惯例。由此，“两票制”政策应该考虑到药品生产流通监管改革的治理方向，并与其相适应。

反对认可国内生产企业设立境内总代理的相关人士则认为，一旦认可国内总代理视同于药品生产企业，在国内生产、流通企业普遍缺乏行业自律和道德约束的实际情况下，过去存在的多级药品代理企业可以采取股权重组的方式组建科工贸一体的销售公司，让总代理公司进行工业开票，规避“两票制”对生产企业责任主体的约束，绕过“两票制”对生产流通环节简化票数的制约，采取利益与风险相隔离的手段，延续过往的底价代理型销售模式，从而实质性架空“两票制”。

example, Merck Serono Company authorizes Squibb Company to manufacture and sell Metformin SR Tablets in China, which returns the domestic distribution rights of Metformin SR Tablets to the Chinese branches of Merck Serono.

② Joint development, and separation of production and distribution rights. For example, Eli Lilly and Company and Hutchison Pharmaceuticals jointly develop the micro-molecular antineoplastic Fruquintinib. Hutchison Pharmaceuticals holds the drug approval number and grants domestic distribution rights to Eli Lilly and Company.

③ Authorization of MAH holder.

④ Overseas production and general agency of import.

⑤ Domestic production and domestic general distributor.

When the Two-invoice System policy was initially implemented, local Two-invoice System policies (including draft) of Chongqing, Yunnan, Guangxi and Hainan provinces (autonomous regions and municipalities) recognized that the commercial enterprise as the sole domestic general agent set up by domestic pharmaceutical manufacturers is deemed as pharmaceutical manufacturer. By November 2017, Chongqing and Yunnan successively waived the relevant provisions and remained consistent with the national version of the system.

There is a major controversy among the local Two-invoice System policies including the parties involved in the relevant industries about recognizing the sole domestic general agent of domestic enterprises as a pharmaceutical manufacturer.

The supporters, including some local officials and scholars, consider that the same market treatment shall be given to domestic enterprises and foreign-funded enterprises in the context of implementing the purchase and sale policy under Two-invoice System across the country. Since the sole importer of foreign-funded enterprises and the sole general agent for overseas production and domestic sale are deemed the same as the manufacturer, the same relevant treatment shall be given to domestic enterprises in line with the general direction of social and economic development. Meanwhile, after the amendment to the *Drug Administration Law*, the system of Marketing Authorization Holder (MAH) is generally implemented in the Chinese pharmaceutical production industry. In the future, the separation of the production and the sale of pharmaceuticals will become a common phenomenon. This is also an international practice. Therefore, the Two-invoice System policy shall take into consideration and adapt to the governance of drug production and distribution regulatory reform.

Those who oppose the establishment of domestic general distributor by domestic production enterprises believe that once domestic general distributor is recognized as the same as pharmaceutical manufacturers at a time when the domestic production and circulation enterprises generally lack industry self-regulation and moral constraints, the previous multi-tier drug agency companies can set up sales company integrating R&D, production and marketing through equity restructuring, so that the general agent can issue invoice for industrial products, circumvent the constraints of the Two-invoice System on the main responsibility of the manufacturers, bypass the limitations of the Two-invoice System on simplified invoicing for production and circulation links, adopt the separation of interests and risks, and continue the previous agency model at the floor price, thus substantially making the Two-invoice System a mere formality.

对于境内生产药品的国内总代理企业是否视同于工业企业，政策发展仍存在不明朗因素，有待继续观察。

2. 流通企业的认定

国家版“两票制”政策对于流通企业开出发票的界定：药品流通集团型企业内部向全资（控股）子公司之间调拨药品可不视为一票，但最多允许开一次发票。

上述界定尚存在多处有待明晰的内容。首先是对于药品流通集团型企业的概念缺乏明确界定，未对流通企业的业务类型、规模等信息作详细表述；其次，未对“调拨”与“销售”概念进行界定；最后，对于“调拨”方向与范围缺乏界定。因此，各地在颁布实施地方版本“两票制”政策时缺乏统一标准，引起政策差异较大，形成政策效果的碎片化。例如，存在下列情形：

①集团型流通企业内部分、子公司的调拨方向不作限制，但仅限于一票（浙江）。

②集团型流通企业内部分、子公司的调拨方向做出限制，但仅限于一票（安徽、湖北）。

3. 允许开出第三票的情形

（1）国家版的相关规定

①为支持建设全国性、区域性的药品物流园区和配送中心，推进药品流通企业仓储资源和运输资源有效整合，多仓协同配送，允许药品流通企业异地建仓，在省域内跨地区使用本企业符合条件的药品仓库。按照远近结合、城乡联动的原则，鼓励支持区域药品配送城乡一体化，打通乡村药品配送“最后一公里”。为特别偏远、交通不便的乡（镇）、村医疗卫生机构配送药品，允许药品流通企业在“两票制”基础上再开一次药品购销发票，以保障基层药品的有效供应。

②内部调拨：药品流通集团型企业内部向全资（控股）子公司或全资（控股）子公司之间调拨药品可不视为一票，但最多允许开一次发票。

（2）地方版的相关规定

地方版本的相关规定见表 1；各省“两票制”政策实施的共性与个性如图 6 所示。

About whether the domestic general distributor which manufactures drugs domestically is regarded as an industrial enterprise, there are still some uncertainties in the development of policies and the jury is still out on the policy.

2. Accreditation of distribution companies

The national version of the Two-invoice System policy defines the invoicing of circulation enterprises as: if drug circulation group-type enterprises allocate drugs to wholly-owned (holding subsidiaries) subsidiaries, it is not deemed as one invoice, but only one invoice is issued at most.

The above definition needs to be clarified in many aspects. First of all, there is a lack of a clear definition of the concept of drug circulation group-type enterprises, without detailed description of the business types and scale of the circulation enterprises. Second, the concept of "allocation" and the "sales" is not defined. Third, the direction and the scope of "allocation" are not defined. Therefore, when promulgating and implementing local versions of the Two-invoice System, there is a lack of uniform standards, resulting in major differences in policies and the fragmented effect of policy. For example, there exist the following situations:

①There is no limit on the allocation direction of subsidiaries and branches in the group-type circulation enterprise, but limited to only one invoice (Zhejiang province).

②There is a limit on the allocation direction of subsidiaries and branches in the group-type circulation enterprise, but limited to only one invoice (Anhui and Hubei provinces).

3. Circumstances under which a third invoice may be issued

(1) Relevant provisions of the national version

①In order to support the construction of national and regional pharmaceutical logistics parks and distribution centers, promote the effective integration of storage resources and transportation resources of pharmaceutical distribution enterprises, and coordinate the distribution from multiple warehouses, drug distribution enterprises are allowed to establish warehouses in different places, and use the drug warehouses of the enterprise in line with conditions in different regions within the same province. In accordance with the principle of consideration to geographical distance and urban-rural linkage, we shall encourage the integration of urban and rural areas in regional drug distribution and link up "the last kilometer" for drug distribution in rural areas. In order to distribute drugs to towns and village medical and health institutions that are especially remote and inaccessible, pharmaceutical distribution enterprises are allowed to issue an invoice for drug purchase and sale on the basis of the Two-invoice System so as to ensure the effective supply of medicines at the community level.

② Internal allocation: if drug circulation group-type enterprises allocate drugs to wholly-owned subsidiaries (holding subsidiaries) or wholly-owned subsidiaries (holding subsidiaries) allocate drugs among themselves, it is not deemed as one invoice, but only one invoice is issued at most.

(2) Relevant provisions of local versions

The relevant provisions of local versions are shown in Table 1; and the similarities and differences of the implementation of the Two-invoice System policy in different provinces are shown in Figure 6.

表 1　地方关于允许开出第三票的规定

安徽	偏远地区：药品经营企业将药品销售到偏远山区基层公立医疗机构的，允许在“两票制”的基础上再开一次药品购销发票，以保障基层药品的有效供应。药品经营企业应在省食品药品监督管理部门备案后实施配送工作
陕西	特殊处理：为确保特殊药品供应，其配送企业不计入数量。偏远地区：乡村相对偏远，医药物流覆盖能力有限，为确保基层用药得到有效保障，暂维持县镇村现有配送模式，适时推行“两票制”
青海	偏远地区：药品流通企业将药品配送到基层医疗机构或边远地区医疗机构的，允许在“两票制”的基础上再开一次药品购销发票，以保障基层药品的有效供应。特殊处理：对发生灾情、疫情、重大事故等突发事件需要应急调拨药品的，应当向省卫生计生委报告
重庆	偏远地区：乡镇（街道）及以下基层医疗卫生机构根据实际情况可增加一票。特殊处理：发生自然灾害、重大疫情、重大突发事件和患者急（抢）救等特殊情况，需要紧急采购药品时，可特殊处理

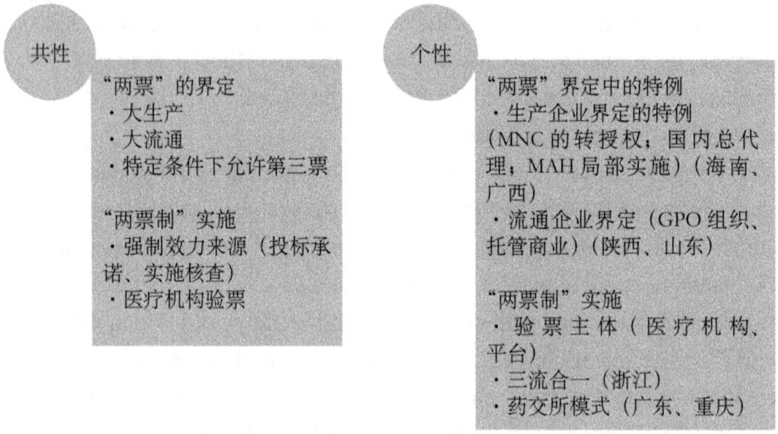

图 6　各省“两票制”政策实施的共性与个性

4. 文件并未明确的相关界定

（1）如何界定流通企业与配送企业的区别

①流通企业

国家版“两票制”细则出台之前，国务院医改办督导处负责人在学术性会议上表示，界定流通企业的原则在于是否有购销行为。依据《药品管理法》（2000 年修订）和《药品经营质量管理规范》（2015 年修订）的相关规定，企业发生药品购销行为的

Table 1 Local regulations on allowing a third invoice to be issued

Anhui	Remote areas: if pharmaceutical trading companies sell medicines to public medical institutions at the community level in remote mountainous areas, it is allowed to issue additional invoice for drug purchase and sale on the basis of the Two-invoice System, ensuring the effective supply of medicines at the community level. Pharmaceutical trading companies shall carry out distribution after registration at the provincial food and drug supervision and administration department
Shaanxi	Special treatment: in order to ensure the supply of special drugs, its delivery enterprises are not included. Remote areas: the rural areas are comparatively remote, wherein the pharmaceutical logistics coverage is limited. The existing delivery model in counties, towns and villages is maintained to ensure the use of medicines at the community level and the Two-invoice System will be implemented in due time
Qinghai	Remote areas: a pharmaceutical distribution enterprise that distributes drugs to primary medical institutions or medical institutions in remote areas is allowed to issue another invoice for medicine purchase and sale based on the Two-invoice System so as to ensure the effective supply of medicines at the community level. Special treatment: in the event of a disaster, outbreak of epidemic, a major accident and other emergencies that require emergency allocation of drugs, it shall be reported to Qinghai Health and Family Planning Commission
Chongqing	Remote areas: medical and health institutions at the township (sub-district) level and below may issue an additional invoice according to the actual situation. Special treatment: in the event of natural disasters, outbreak of epidemic, major emergencies and first aid (emergency treatment) of patients that require emergency procurement of drugs, it is treated according to special regulations

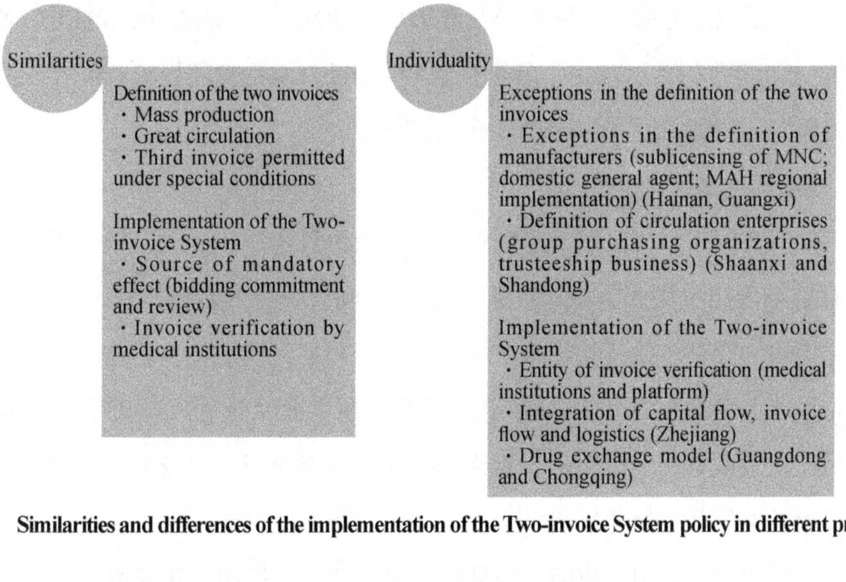

Figure 6 Similarities and differences of the implementation of the Two-invoice System policy in different provinces

4. Definitions not clearly stipulated in the documents

(1) How to define the difference between circulation enterprises and delivery enterprises

①Circulation enterprises

Before the promulgation of the detailed rules on the state version of the Two-invoice System, the head of the Supervisory Office of the Medical Reform Office of the State Council said at an academic conference that the principle of defining a circulation enterprise lies in whether there is an

界定是，除了发生商业意义上的购进和销出行为外，应具备相应资质并存在满足上述药品监管法规所要求的药品采购、验收、仓储保管、运输分发和销售服务等实际业务，并严格执行《药品经营质量管理规范》所要求的“货票同行”“货票账款一一对应”等法规要求，同时，相关企业应具备完备的药品质量追溯和风险管理体系并切实履行职责。

②配送服务型企业

通常认为，药品配送企业指经过药品集中采购部门认可的负责当地药品配送的医药商业公司或物流公司。《药品招标工作规范》第十九条规定：“药品生产企业作为投标人，其中标品种可以由生产企业直接配送，也可以委托批发企业或者其他物流企业代理配送。”根据这一规定，药品批发企业、药品生产企业和其他物流企业都可以承担中标药品的配送任务。为医疗机构提供了更多的选择配送企业的机会，也为各种物流资源通过集中招标采购进入药品流通市场提供了机会。

不论国家版或地方版的“两票制”政策均未明确界定药品购销和配送二者间“费用率”或“加价率”的合适范围，是否按照《药品经营质量管理规范》和《药品管理法》来做相关界定，“两票制”相关政策应予以明确。

（2）集团型流通企业的认定

现有政策文件未对集团型流通企业的概念做出界定。传统上，根据组成集团的成员组织数量来界定“集团”概念，但并没有从成员企业的数量、销售规模、经营品种数量和销售额等具体数值指标来做界定。鉴于药品经营的特点常常为品类复杂，品种、规格众多，货值较高，如何界定集团型流通企业及合乎成员资质的客观指标要求，应当在相关政策中予以明确。否则，行业中可能会衍生出较多游走于法规边缘的灰色、边缘类型的药品经营集团，引发更多的行业无序现象。

通常，依据行业惯例，我国集团型药品流通企业包括如下几种类型：

传统意义上的4家全国性流通企业（国药、上药、华润、九州通）；区域龙头商业企业（如南京医药、广州医药、瑞康、浙江英特）。

act of purchase or sale. Pursuant to the relevant provisions of the *Drug Administration Law* (2000 amendment) and *Good Supply Practice for Pharmaceutical Products* (2015 amendment), an enterprise is defined as an entity having the act of purchase and sale of drugs if, in addition to the business purchase and sale activities, the enterprise has the corresponding qualifications and has actual business such as drug procurement, acceptance, storage and transportation, distribution and sales services as required by the aforesaid drug administration law, and strictly implements the provisions of the *Good Supply Practice for Pharmaceutical Products* pertaining to "goods accompanied by invoice", and "correspondence among goods, invoices and accounts". At the same time, relevant enterprises shall put in place complete drug quality traceability and risk management system and fulfill their duties.

②Delivery service-oriented enterprises

It is generally considered that a pharmaceutical delivery company refers to a pharmaceutical commercial company or a logistics company responsible for the delivery of medicines in local area that has been approved by the agency in charge of centralized drug procurement. Article 19 of the *Specifications on Drug Bidding* stipulates that "if a drug manufacturer is a bidder, the varieties that win the bidding can be delivered directly by the manufacturer, or delivered by the entrusted wholesaling enterprise or other logistics business agent." According to this regulation, the drug wholesaling enterprises, drug manufacturers and other logistics companies can assume the delivery of the drugs that win the bidding. This provides medical institutions with more opportunities to choose the delivery enterprises, and provides opportunities for various logistics resources to enter the pharmaceutical circulation market through centralized purchasing by invitation to bid.

Neither the national version nor local versions of the Two-invoice System policy clearly define the appropriate range of "cost rates" or "markup percentage" among purchase, sale and delivery of pharmaceuticals. The policy related to the Two-invoice System shall stipulate whether the definition is made according to the *Good Supply Practice for Pharmaceutical Products* and the *Drug Administration Law*.

(2) Accreditation of group-type circulation enterprises

The existing policy document does not define the concept of group-type circulation enterprises. Traditionally, the concept of "group" is defined according to the number of member organizations of a group, but it is not defined by specific numerical indicators such as the number of member enterprises, the sales scale, the number of products for business and the sales volume. Given fact that the operations of pharmaceuticals are often characterized by complex types, extensive varieties and specifications and high value, the objective indicators of how to define group-type distribution enterprises and the qualifications of members shall be clarified in relevant policies. Otherwise, it may trigger more gray and marginalized drug business groups that are on the verge of violation of laws and regulations, leading to greater disorder in the industry.

According to industry practice, the group-type pharmaceutical circulation enterprises in China generally include the following types:

The four national circulation enterprises (Sinopharm, Shanghai Pharma, CR Pharmaceutical, and Jointown Pharmaceutical) in a traditional sense; and the regional leading commercial enterprises (such as Nanjing Pharmaceutical, Guangzhou Pharmaceuticals, Realcan, and INT'L Group).

上述两类集团型流通企业的总公司，与它们的分、子公司共同构成集团型流通企业。这些集团型的流通企业与其分、子公司之间是否严格限定于绝对控股？相对控股是否排除在外？

除了上述医药流通企业以外，还有哪些商业企业可以被视同于集团型流通企业？

国内省级代理企业与地市二级、三级代理企业重组成为医药商业企业集团的类型，是否能视作该类型？流通企业仅依据股权关系构成集团、业务缺乏共同交集的情形，是否能视作集团型流通企业？

上述问题均为对集团型流通企业认定中需要明确的概念。

（3）集团型流通企业内部调拨行为认定

不论在国家版还是各省的药品购销“两票制”政策中均在一定程度上认可内部商品调拨行为。但商品调拨行为的定性是什么？加价率多少为适宜的调拨费率？怎么区别于销售加价？

据调查，国药控股系统内，部分企业间调拨的加价率通常为 2% ～ 3%，但并没有严格限定具体的数字，通常将成本性的加成视作调拨，而不同经营管理水平及规模的企业，商品调拨的成本有高低之分，现实运行中亦缺乏对调拨效率高低认定的技术评价标准。

同样，对购销行为的最低加价率也缺乏明确的界定。

而官员对于药品购销“两票制”的约束对象定性为控制发生销售行为的次数通常不超过 2 次，特殊情形允许 3 次，但对委托配送服务的次数则不作限制，满足药品供应保障目标即可。

（五）各省（区、市）“两票制”实施情况

各地出台“两票制”执行方案及全面执行时间见表 2。

The head office of the above two types of group circulation enterprises, together with their branches and subsidiaries, constitute group circulation enterprises. Are these group-type circulation enterprises and its branches and subsidiaries strictly limited to absolute shareholding? Is relatively shareholding excluded?

In addition to the above pharmaceutical circulation companies, what other commercial enterprises can be regarded as group circulation enterprises?

Whether the pharmaceutical commercial enterprise groups resulting from the reorganization of domestic provincial-level agency enterprises and municipal secondary or third-level agency enterprises can be regarded as this type? Whether circulation enterprises can be regarded as a group circulation enterprise when circulation enterprises constitute the group based on equity only, without overlapping business?

The above problems need to be clarified for clear understanding of the group circulation enterprises.

(3) Accreditation of internal allocation among group circulation enterprises

Both the national and the local drug purchase and sale policies under the Two-invoice System recognize the act of internal allocation of goods to some extent. However, how is the nature of the allocation of goods defined? How much the markup percentage is the appropriate rate of allocation fees? How to distinguish it from sales markup?

According to the survey, the markup percentage for allocations among some enterprises within Sinopharm Holding system is usually 2%~3%. However, it is not strictly limited to the specific figures. The cost markup is generally regarded as allocation and enterprises with different levels of operation and management and scale have different costs of commodity allocation. There is a lack of technical evaluation criteria for the accreditation of allocation efficiency in actual operation.

Similarly, there is a lack of a clear definition of the minimum markup percentage for purchase and sale.

Officials restrict the sales activities under the drug purchase and sale under the Two-invoice System is usually twice, or three times under special circumstances. But the number of commissioned delivery service is not limited, so as to meet the guarantee of drug supply.

(V) Implementation of the Two-invoice System in different provinces (autonomous regions and municipalities)

Table 2 is the list of the implementation programs and the schedule of full implementation of the Two-invoice System in different regions.

表 2　各地出台“两票制”执行方案及全面执行时间一览

地区	对“两票制”的态度	公文号 / 名称	全面执行日
全国	争取 2018 年在全国范围推开	国办发〔2017〕13 号；国医改办发〔2016〕4 号	2018 年年底
江西	2017 年 4 月 14 日启动实施，2017 年先行在南昌、吉安、赣州、抚州等 4 个公立医院改革试点城市推行“两票制”，争取到 2018 年在全省全面推开，每个药械品种的一级经销商不得超过 2 个	赣卫药政字〔2017〕8 号	未有确定期限
甘肃	分医院级别阶段实施。三级公立医院须于 2017 年 10 月 1 日起全面贯彻落实“两票制”；全省二级公立医疗机构须于新一轮药品集中采购中标结果执行起全面落实“两票制”，2018 年在底前落实到位	《公立医疗机构药品采购“两票制”实施方案（试行）》	未有确定期限
新疆	未有明确专门公文界定	《关于加强自治区公立医院药品集中采购工作的实施意见》	未有确定期限
西藏	未有明确专门公文界定	《西藏自治区公立医疗卫生机构药品集中采购实施方案（2016 版）》	未有确定期限
青海	部分实施。2016 年 12 月 15 日起对目前全省执行的中标药品中，具有直采和一级代理的药品品种实行“两票制”，原配送企业不变。各级公立医疗机构也要优先选择能够实行直采和一级代理的医用耗材生产企业和流通企业，逐步提高配送集中度	《关于青海省公立医疗机构药品采购实行“两票制”的实施意见（试行）》 《关于药品和医用耗材推行“两票制”有关事项的通知》	未有确定期限

Table 2 List of the implementation programs and the schedule of full implementation of the Two-invoice System in different regions

Region	Attitude to the Two-invoice System	File No. / full name	Date of full implementation
Nationwide	Launch the nationwide promote in 2018 as far as possible	GBF〔2017〕No.13; GYGBF〔2016〕No. 4	At the end of 2018
Jiangxi	Kicked off implementation on April 14, 2017, and implemented the Two-invoice System in four pilot cities for the reform of public hospitals including Nanchang, Ji'an, Ganzhou and Fuzhou in 2017, and promote this in the entire province by 2018; at most 2 first-level distributors for each variety of medical instruments	GWYZZ〔2017〕No. 8	Undetermined deadline
Gansu	Stage implementation by the levels of hospitals. Tertiary public hospitals must fully implement the Two-invoice System as from October 1, 2017; all the second-class public medical institutions in Gansu province must fully implement the Two-invoice System as from the execution of the results of winning the bid in a new round of the centralized procurement of drugs and put it in place by the end of 2018	*Implementation Plan of the Two-invoice System to Be Adopted in the Drug Procurement of Public Medical Institutions (for trial implementation)*	Undetermined deadline
Xinjiang	Not clearly defined by specific documents	*Implementation Opinions on the Centralized Procurement of Medicines of Public Medical Institutions in Autonomous Regions*	Undetermined deadline
Tibet	Not clearly defined by specific documents	*Implementation Plan of the Centralized Procurement of Medicines of the Public Medical Institutions in Tibet Autonomous Region (2016)*	Undetermined deadline
Qinghai	Partial implementation. From December 15, 2016 onwards, Two-invoice System is adopted for the varieties of medicines that have direct procurement and first-class agency for the drugs among successful bidding in the province, and the original delivery enterprises remain unchanged. Public medical institutions at all levels shall also give priority to the selection of medical consumables manufacturers and distribution enterprises that can adopt direct procurement and first-class agency, and gradually increase distribution concentration	*Implementation Opinions on the Two-invoice System to Be Adopted in the Drug Procurement of the Public Medical Institutions in Qinghai Province (for trial implementation)* *Notice on the Relevant Matters of the Two-invoice System to Be Adopted in the Purchase and Sales of Medicines and Medical Consumables*	Undetermined deadline

续表

地区	对“两票制”的态度	公文号 / 名称	全面执行日
贵州	完全照搬国家版“两票制”文件，不做任何调整，无执行的时间点	《印发关于在公立医疗机构药品采购中推行“两票制”的实施意见（试行）的通知》	未有确定期限
云南	分阶段开展。自 2017 年 10 月 1 日起，云南的 6 个医改试点城市（昆明、玉溪、红河州、普洱市、曲靖市、大理州）的三级公立医院率先推行“两票制”，2018 年 7 月 6 个医改试点城市全面推行，二级及以下公立医疗机构有 9 个月过渡期，在此期间允许再开一票，2018 年 10 月开始全省将全面推行“两票制”	《云南省公立医疗机构药品采购中推行“两票制”的实施方案（试行）》	2018 年 10 月 1 日
河南	2017 年 12 月 31 日前，洛阳、焦作、濮阳、鹤壁、漯河、三门峡等 6 个公立医院综合改革试点城市所有公立医疗机构实行“两票制”，2018 年 6 月底前，力争其他省辖市、直管县（市）公立医疗机构全面实行“两票制”。短缺药品、临床必需但使用量较小的药品可以暂不实行“两票制”，偏远地区可再开一票	《河南省公立医疗机构药品采购推行“两票制”实施意见（试行）》	2018 年 6 月 30 日
广东	自 2017 年 12 月 2 日实施，过渡期 6 个月。2018 年 6 月 1 日全省公立医院（深圳试点 GPO 采购，除外）全面实施；50 多个山区县乡镇医疗机构（不含社区卫生服务中心）可再开一票	《关于医疗机构药品交易“两票制”的实施方案（试行）》	2018 年 6 月 1 日
广西	2017 年 9 月 1 日起，柳州、玉林、桂林、百色及防城港市 5 个试点城市率先实施“两票制”，其他区市 2018 年 1 月 1 日起全面执行，不另设过渡期；全国总代理可视为药品生产企业	桂医改办〔2017〕18 号	2018 年 1 月 1 日

Continued

Region	Attitude to the Two-invoice System	File No. / full name	Date of full implementation
Guizhou	Copy the national version of the Two-invoice System, without any adjustment or implementation time	*Notice on the Printing and Distribution of the Implementation Opinions on the Two-invoice System to Be Adopted in the Drug Procurement of Public Medical Institutions (for trial implementation)*	Undetermined deadline
Yunnan	Carry out in stages. Starting from October 1, 2017, tertiary public hospitals in the six pilot cities for the medical reform in Yunnan (Kunming, Yuxi, Honghe, Pu'er, Qujing and Dali) took the lead in implementing the Two-invoice System. In July 2018, it will be fully implemented in the six pilot cities for medical reform. There will be a nine-month transitional period for public medical institutions at the second level and below. Additional invoice can be issued during this period. Starting from October 2018, the province will fully implement the Two-invoice System	*Implementation Plan of the Two-invoice System to Be Adopted in the Drug Procurement of the Public Medical Institutions in Yunnan Province (for trial implementation)*	October 1, 2018
Henan	Before December 31, 2017, all public medical institutions in the six pilot cities of comprehensive reform of public hospitals including Luoyang, Jiaozuo, Puyang, Hebi, Luohe and Sanmenxia will implement Two-invoice System. All public medical institutions in other provincially administered municipalities and counties (cities) directly under the province government fully implement the Two-invoice System by the end of June, 2018. The Two-invoice System is not implemented for the time being for inadequate drugs and drugs that are clinically necessary but require little dosage. Additional invoice may be issued in remote areas	*Implementation Plan of the Two-invoice System to Be Adopted in the Drug Procurement of the Public Medical Institutions in Henan Province (for trial implementation)*	June 30, 2018
Guangdong	From December 2, 2017, the Two-invoice System was launched, and there is a 6-month transitional period. All public hospitals in the province implement the system on June 1, 2018 (except Shenzhen that implements GPO procurement on a pilot basis). More than 50 medical institutions (excluding community health centers) in mountainous counties and towns can issue an additional invoice	*Implementation Plan of the Two-invoice System to Be Adopted in the Drug Procurement of Public Medical Institutions (for trail implementation)*	June 1, 2018
Guangxi	From September 1, 2017, the five pilot cities of Liuzhou, Yulin, Guilin, Baise and Fangchenggang took the lead in the implementation of the Two-invoice System. The other districts and cities will fully implement the system on January 1, 2018 and no transitional period is provided. The national general distributor can be regarded as the pharmaceutical manufacturer	GYGB〔2017〕No. 18	January 1, 2018

续表

地区	对“两票制”的态度	公文号 / 名称	全面执行日
宁夏	过渡期为 2017 年 6—8 月，8 月新招投标药品、谈判药品、基础输液和国家定点生产药品实现“两票制”，2018 年 1 月宁夏公立医院挂网药品实现“两票制”	宁药招办发〔2017〕16 号	2018 年 1 月 1 日
山东	2017 年 11 月 1 日前，济南、滨州、青岛、潍坊、威海、东营等 6 个医改试点城市率先执行“两票制”；2018 年 1 月 1 日起，其他各市都要执行“两票制”；在试点城市三级甲等综合医院选择部分用量较大、市场供应渠道简单的药品实行“一票制”	《山东省公立医疗机构药品采购推行“两票制”实施方案（试行）》	2018 年 1 月 1 日
湖北	2017 年 6 月 9 日起，在全省所有公立医疗机构药品采购中启动实施“两票制”，2017 年 12 月 31 日前为过渡期，2018 年 1 月 1 日起全省公立医疗机构正式全面实施“两票制”，视为生产企业的，需向医疗机构做出书面说明，同时要提供生产企业开具的发票复印件（加盖生产企业的公章）；偏远山区需备案，可再开一票	《全省公立医院医疗机构药品采购“两票制”实施方案（试行）》	2018 年 1 月 1 日
江苏	全省各级公立医疗机构（包含基层医疗卫生机构和村卫生室）全部实施，第二批集采药品自采购结果执行日期实施，第一批已上网的急抢救类、妇儿专科非专利药须于 2017 年 12 月 31 日前全面执行“两票制”	《江苏省公立医疗机构药品采购推行“两票制”实施方案（征求意见稿）》 苏医改办发〔2017〕12 号	2017 年 12 月 31 日
上海	全市所有公立医疗机构药品采购全部实行“两票制”；配送到郊区医疗卫生服务站点（村卫生室）的药品，允许再开一票	沪人社医〔2017〕246 号	2017 年 12 月 31 日

Continued

Region	Attitude to the Two-invoice System	File No. / full name	Date of full implementation
Ningxia	The transitional period is from June to August in 2017; in August, the Two-invoice System is implemented for drugs under new bidding, drugs with negotiated prices, basic infusion and drugs for state designated production; in January 2018, public hospitals in Ningxia adopt the Two-invoice System for drugs for online bidding	NYZBF〔2017〕No. 16	January 1, 2018
Shandong	Before November 1, 2017, the six pilot cities for medical reform including Jinan, Binzhou, Qingdao, Weifang, Weihai and Dongying took the lead in implementing the Two-invoice System. As from January 1, 2018, other cities shall implement the Two-invoice System. In the pilot cities, the One-invoice System is implemented for some drugs with high dosage and simple market supply channels at Grade 3, Class A general hospitals	*Implementation Plan of the Two-invoice System to Be Adopted in the Drug Procurement of the Public Medical Institutions in Shandong Province (for trial implementation)*	January 1, 2018
Hubei	From June 9, 2017, the Two-invoice System was launched in all public medical institutions in the province for drug procurement. The period before December 31, 2017 is the transitional period. As from January 1, 2018, the public medical institutions in the province officially kick off the Two-invoice System. Institutions regarded as manufacturing enterprises must make a written explanation to the medical institution and provide a copy of the invoice issued by the manufacturer (affixed with the official seal of the manufacturer); additional invoice may be issued on the condition of filing in remote mountainous areas	*Implementation Plan of the Two-invoice System to Be Adopted in the Drug Procurement of the Public Medical Institutions in Hubei Province (for trial implementation)*	January 1, 2018
Jiangsu	It was implemented at public medical institutions at all levels in Jiangsu Province (including primary medical and health institutions and village clinics). The second batch of the centralized procurement of drugs was implemented as from the implementation date of the procurement results. The Two-invoice System must be fully implemented for the first batch of generic drugs for emergency rescue and gynecology and pediatrics purposes for online purchase before December 31, 2017	*Implementation Plan of the Two-invoice System to Be Adopted in the Drug Procurement of the Public Medical Institutions in Jiangsu Province (draft)* SYGBF〔2017〕No. 12	December 31, 2017
Shanghai	The Two-invoice System is implemented for purchases of medicines by all public medical institutions in Shanghai. Additional invoice may be issued for drugs delivered to the suburban medical and health service sites (village clinics)	HRSY〔2017〕No. 246	December 31, 2017

续表

地区	对“两票制”的态度	公文号 / 名称	全面执行日
浙江	2017 年 8 月 1 日起实施，过渡期至 2017 年 10 月 31 日。本省所有的公立医疗机构都需要执行“两票制”	浙卫发〔2017〕47 号	2017 年 11 月 1 日
内蒙古	2017 年 7 月 1 日启动“两票制”工作，给予 4 个月的过渡期，2017 年 11 月 1 日，全区公立医疗机构（含基层医疗卫生机构）全部实行“两票制”	内卫计规范〔2017〕5 号	2017 年 11 月 1 日
海南	2017 年 5 月 1 日起启动实施，2017 年 9 月 30 日前为过渡期。2017 年 11 月 1 日起，全省所有公立医疗机构全面实施“两票制”。特别偏远的乡镇卫生院由市县卫生计生委（卫生局）报省卫生计生委备案，另行规定；高值耗材暂不执行	《海南省公立医疗机构药品采购“两票制”实施细则（试行）》	2017 年 11 月 1 日
湖南	2017 年 4 月 1 日起实施，9 月 30 日前为过渡期，10 月 1 日起全省所有公立医疗机构药品采购全面实行“两票制”，偏远山区可再开一票	《湖南省公立医疗机构药品采购“两票制”实施方案（试行）》	2017 年 10 月 1 日
吉林	2017 年 6 月 30 日起，正式启动实施“两票制”，暂定 9 月 30 日后全部实行“两票制”，边境县（区）、国家级及省级贫困县辖区内政府办基层医疗卫生机构，允许再开一票。合理控制配送企业数量，非基层医疗机构原则上不超过 15 家	《吉林省公立医疗机构药品采购“两票制”实施方案》 吉卫联发〔2017〕55 号	2017 年 9 30 日
四川	2017 年 4 月 6 日起，全省公立医疗机构（除民族贫困边远地区公立医疗机构和其他地区基层医疗机构外）全面实行“两票制”。给予 5 个月的过渡时间	《关于在四川省公立医疗机构药品采购中推行“两票制”的实施方案（试行）》	2017 年 9 月 6 日

Continued

Region	Attitude to the Two-invoice System	File No. / full name	Date of full implementation
Zhejiang	It was implemented from August 1, 2017. The transitional period lasts until October 31, 2017. All public medical institutions in the province need to implement the Two-invoice System	ZWF 〔2017〕 No. 47	November 1, 2017
Inner Mongolia	The Two-invoice System was launched on July 1, 2017. There is a 4-month transitional period. On November 1, 2017, the region's public health institutions (including primary health care institutions) all implement the Two-invoice System	NWJGF 〔2017〕 No. 5	November 1, 2017
Hainan	It was implemented as from May 1, 2017. The period before September 30, 2017 is the transitional period. Since November 1, 2017, all public medical institutions in the province fully implement the Two-invoice System. Special provisions apply to township health centers in highly remote areas after the county health and family planning commission (Health Bureau) has reported to the Provincial health and family planning commission for the record; it is not implemented for the time being for high value consumables	*Implementation Rules of the Two-invoice System to Be Adopted in the Drug Procurement of the Public Medical Institutions in Hainan Province (for trial implementation)*	November 1, 2017
Hunan	It entered into force on April 1, 2017 and the period before September 30 is the transitional period. As from October 1, the Two-invoice System will be fully implemented for drug procurement by all public medical institutions in the province. Additional invoice applies in remote mountain areas	*Implementation Plan of the Two-invoice System to Be Adopted in the Drug Procurement of the Public Medical Institutions in Hunan Province (for trial implementation)*	October 1, 2017
Jilin	Since June 30, 2017, Two-invoice System was officially launched. It is tentatively decided that the Two-invoice System is implemented after September 30. The government-run primary medical and health institutions in border counties (districts), and national and provincial poverty-stricken counties may issue an additional invoice. The number of delivery companies may be kept at a reasonable level. The number of non-primary medical institutions does not exceed 15 in principle	*Implementation Plan of the Two-invoice System to Be Adopted in the Drug Procurement of the Public Medical Institutions in Jilin Province* JWLF 〔2017〕 No. 55	September 30, 2017
Sichuan	Since April 6, 2017, public medical institutions in the province, except public medical institutions in remote poverty-stricken areas inhabited by ethnic minorities and primary medical institutions in other regions, have fully implemented the Two-invoice System. There is a 5-month transitional period	*Implementation Plan of the Two-invoice System to Be Adopted in the Drug Procurement of the Public Medical Institutions in Sichuan Province (for trial implementation)*	September 6, 2017

续表

地区	对“两票制”的态度	公文号 / 名称	全面执行日
黑龙江	2017 年 9 月 1 日起，正式全面实施“两票制”，2017 年 8 月 31 日前为过渡期。全省所有公立医疗机构（含基层医疗机构，村卫生室药品由乡镇卫生院代购）全部实行“两票制”，鼓励其他医疗机构推行“两票制”。特别偏远、交通不便的乡镇及以下基层医疗卫生机构可增加一票	《关于印发黑龙江省公立医疗机构药品采购“两票制”实施方案（试行）的通知》	2017 年 9 月 1 日
辽宁	2017 年 6 月 1 日起，全省各级公立医疗机构启动“两票制”，2017 年 9 月 1 日全面实施“两票制”	《辽宁省公立医疗机构药品采购“两票制”实施细则（试行）》	2017 年 9 月 1 日
天津	2017 年 9 月 1 日起，全市公立医院（包括政府办基层医疗机构）全部执行“两票制”；对 13 大类高值耗材执行“两票制”	《天津市公立医疗机构药品采购推行“两票制”实施方案（试行）》津医改办发〔2017〕1 号	2017 年 9 月 1 日
山西	2017 年 5 月 1 日起启动实施“两票制”。2017 年 7 月 31 日前为过渡期。2017 年 8 月 1 日起，全省公立医疗机构采购药品全面实行“两票制”，不得委托科技公司、咨询公司等非药品经营企业在我省推广销售药品（CSO）	《山西省推行公立医疗机构药品采购“两票制”实施方案（试行）》	2017 年 8 月 1 日
重庆	2016 年 12 月 31 日起启动实施“两票制”。2017 年 5 月 31 日前为过渡期，2017 年 6 月 1 日起，全市所有公立医疗机构正式全面实施“两票制”，配送企业数量应进行合理控制；区县需增加一票的需公开遴选确定经营企业并进行备案	《重庆市公立医疗机构药品采购“两票制”实施方案（试行）》	2017 年 6 月 1 日

Continued

Region	Attitude to the Two-invoice System	File No. / full name	Date of full implementation
Heilongjiang	The Two-invoice System was fully implemented on September 1, 2017 and the period before August 31, 2017 is the transitional period. All public medical institutions in the province (including primary medical institutions; the drugs for village clinics are procured by township hospitals) implement the Two-invoice System and other medical institutions are encouraged to implement the Two-invoice System. An additional invoice may be issued by primary medical institutions in particularly remote townships and villages with poor traffic network	*Notice on the Printing and Distribution of the Implementation Plan of the Two-invoice System to Be Adopted in the Drug Procurement of the Public Medical Institutions in Heilongjiang Province (for trial implementation)*	September 1, 2017
Liaoning	From June 1, 2017, the Two-invoice System was launched by public medical institutions at all levels across the province. The Two-invoice System was fully implemented on September 1, 2017	*Implementation Rules of the Two-invoice System to Be Adopted in the Drug Procurement of the Public Medical Institutions in Liaoning Province (for trail implementation)*	September 1, 2017
Tianjin	From September 1, 2017, public hospitals in the city (including government-run primary medical institutions) fully implement the Two-invoice System; the Two-invoice System is implemented for 13 categories of high-value consumables	*Implementation Plan of the Two-invoice System to Be Adopted in the Drug Procurement of the Public Medical Institutions in Tianjin (for trial implementation)* JYGBF〔2017〕No. 1	September 1, 2017
Shanxi	The Two-invoice System was launched on May 1, 2017. The transitional period lasts until July 31, 2017. Since August 1, 2017, public medical institutions in the province have fully implemented the Two-invoice System for the procurement of drugs, and may not entrust non-drug trading companies such as technology companies and consulting companies to promote the sale of drugs in the province (CSO)	*Implementation Plan of the Two-invoice System to Be Adopted in the Drug Procurement of the Public Medical Institutions in Shanxi Province (for trial implementation)*	August 1, 2017
Chongqing	The Two-invoice System was put into practice on December 31, 2016. The period before May 31, 2017 is the transitional period. As from June 1, 2017, all public medical institutions in the city formally implement the Two-invoice System and the number of delivery enterprises shall be rationally controlled; if an additional invoice is required, business enterprises in districts and counties are selected in an open manner and filed for the record	*Implementation Plan of the Two-invoice System to Be Adopted in the Drug Procurement of the Public Medical Institutions in Chongqing (for trial implementation)*	June 1, 2017

续表

地区	对“两票制”的态度	公文号 / 名称	全面执行日
河北	2017 年 5 月 1 日起全省公立医疗机构药品采购中推行“两票制”，麻醉药品、第一类精神药品、计划生育药品、计划免疫药品、中药饮片，可不执行“两票制”	《河北省公立医疗机构药品采购推行“两票制”实施方案（征求意见稿）》	2017 年 5 月 1 日
北京	2017 年 4 月 8 日实施“两票制”	《医药分开综合改革实施方案》	2017 年 4 月 8 日
陕西	2017 年 1 月 1 日起全面实施“两票制”。限定药品、耗材配送商数量：三级医院药品器械配送商不超过 15 家，二级医院药品配送商不超过 5 家、器械配送商不超过 15 家。配送商由药企在医疗机构确定的企业中选择。医用耗材实行“两票制”确有困难的，可先在高值医用耗材中实施（明确耗材“两票制”）	陕医改办发〔2016〕8 号 陕政发〔2016〕26 号	2017 年 1 月 1 日
安徽	2016 年 11 月 1 日起全省公立医院全面执行“两票制”，偏远山区允许再开一票	皖食药监药化流〔2016〕37 号	2016 年 11 月 1 日
福建	2009 年开始，开始在全省药品采购供应工作中执行“两票制”制度。2014 年，限定配送商数量：基药配送集中到 10 个配送商，非基药 11 家；取消分片区配送模式，实行全省统一配送。严格实行“两票制”政策	《福建省 2014 年医疗机构药品集中招标采购实施意见》	2014 年 7 月

资料来源：各省市政府网站、联讯证券研究院。

（六）部分省市出台器械耗材“两票制”执行方案

虽然国家层面还未出台具体器械耗材“两票制”文件方案，但部分省市对耗材“两票制”也有明确执行方案，以陕西为代表，耗材“两票制”伴随药品“两票制”，全省推广，限定耗材配送商数量，三级医院不超过 15 家，二级医院药品不超过 5 家、器械不超过 15 家。配送商由药企在医疗机构确定的企业中选择。医用耗材实行“两

Continued

Region	Attitude to the Two-invoice System	File No. / full name	Date of full implementation
Hebei	Public medical institutions in the province implemented the Two-invoice System for drug procurement on May 1, 2017. The Two-invoice System is not required for narcotic drugs, psychotropic substances in category I, family planning drugs, planned immunization drugs and Chinese medicine decoction pieces	*Implementation Plan of the Two-invoice System to Be Adopted in the Drug Procurement of the Public Medical Institutions in Hebei Province (draft)*	May 1, 2017
Beijing	The Two-invoice System was implemented on April 8, 2017	*Implementation Plan of the Comprehensive Reform on the Separation of Clinic from Pharmacy*	April 8, 2017
Shaanxi	The Two-invoice System was fully implemented on January 1, 2017. The number of distributors of limited drugs and consumables: not more than 15 for tertiary hospitals; not more than 5 for secondary hospitals for drugs, and not more than 15 for medical instruments. Distributors are selected by pharmaceutical companies from enterprises determined by medical institutions. If it is really hard to implement the Two-invoice System for medical consumables, it can be implemented for high-value medical consumables (Stipulate the Two-invoice System for consumables)	SYGBF 〔2016〕 No. 8 SZF 〔2016〕 No. 26	January 1, 2017
Anhui	Public hospitals in the province fully implemented the Two-invoice System on November 1, 2016. An additional invoice is allowed in remote mountainous areas	WSYJYHL 〔2016〕 No. 37	November 1, 2016
Fujian	Since 2009, the Two-invoice System was implemented for drug procurement and supply in the province. In 2014, the number of distributors was limited: 10 distributors for essential medicines and 11 for non-essential drugs; the zone-based delivery mode was cancelled, and the province-wide centralized delivery was implemented. The Two-invoice System policy is strictly enforced	*Implementation Opinions on the Centralized Procurement of Medicines by Means of Bidding of Public Medical Institutions in Fujian Province in 2014*	July, 2014

Source: Provincial and municipal government websites, and Lianxun Securities Research Institute.

(VI) Some provinces and cities introduced the Two-invoice System implementation program for equipment consumables

Although the State has not yet introduced a program for the Two-invoice System for equipment consumables, some provinces and cities promulgate clear implementation program for the Two-invoice System. Shaanxi is the representative; the Two-invoice System for consumables is promoted in the province alongside the Two-invoice System for drugs. The number of distributors of consumables is

票制”确有困难的，可先在高值医用耗材中实施。另外，天津也在“两票制”执行方案中明确对13类高值耗材在全市执行“两票制”；青海和江苏部分地市（泰州、启东、南京）也出台（高值）耗材“两票制”采购方案。

目前，“两票制”全国执行尚集中在药品领域，器械耗材“两票制”仅在部分省市有推行（表3）。各地“两票制”实施情况见表4。

表3　宣布执行器械耗材“两票制”的地区一览

地区	对“两票制”的态度	公文号 / 名称	全面执行日
陕西	2017年1月1日起全面实施。限定药品、耗材配送商数量：三级医院不超过15家，二级医院药品不超过5家、器械不超过15家。配送商由药企在医疗机构确定的企业中选择。医用耗材实行“两票制”确有困难的，可先在高值医用耗材中实施（明确耗材“两票制”）	陕医改办发〔2016〕8号、陕政发〔2016〕26号	2017年1月1日
天津	2017年9月1日起，全市公立医院（包括政府办基层医疗机构）全部执行“两票制”；对13大类高值耗材执行“两票制”	《天津市公立医疗机构药品和医用耗材采购推行“两票制”实施方案（试行）》津医改办发〔2017〕1号	2017年9月1日
青海	部分实施。2016年12月15日起对目前全省执行的中标药品中，具有直采和一级代理的药品品种实行“两票制”，原配送企业不变。各级公立医疗机构也要优先选择能够实行直采和一级代理的医用耗材生产企业和流通企业，逐步提高配送集中度	《关于青海省公立医疗机构药品采购实行“两票制”的实施意见（试行）》《关于药品和医用耗材推行“两票制”有关事项的通知》	未有明确时间表

limited: not more than 15 for tertiary hospitals; not more than 5 for secondary hospitals for drugs, and not more than 15 for medical instruments. Distributors are selected by pharmaceutical companies from enterprises determined by medical institutions. If it is really hard to implement the Two-invoice System for medical consumables, it can be implemented for high-value medical consumables. In addition, Tianjin also implements the Two-invoice System for 13 categories of high-value consumables. The Two-invoice System has also been introduced for procurement program of (high-value) consumables in some cities in Qinghai and Jiangsu (Taizhou, Qidong and Nanjing).

At present, the Two-invoice System implementation is still concentrated in the pharmaceutical field, and the Two-invoice System for equipment consumables is only implemented in some provinces and cities (Table 3). Table 4 shows the Two-invoice System implementation in different regions.

Table 3 List of the regions that announce the implementation of the Two-invoice System

Region	Attitude to the Two-invoice System	File No./full name	Date of full implementation
Shaanxi	Full implementation since January 1, 2017. The number of distributors of drugs and consumables is limited: not more than 15 for tertiary hospitals; not more than 5 for secondary hospitals for drugs, and not more than 15 for medical instruments. Distributors are selected by pharmaceutical companies from the enterprises determined by medical institutions. If it is really hard to implement the Two-invoice System for medical consumables, it can be implemented for high-value medical consumables (Stipulate Two-invoice System for consumables)	SYGBF〔2016〕No. 8 SZF〔2016〕No. 26	January 1, 2017
Tianjin	From September 1, 2017, public hospitals in the city (including government-run primary medical institutions) fully implement the Two-invoice System; the Two-invoice System is implemented for 13 categories of high-value consumables	*Implementation Plan of the Two-invoice System to Be Adopted in the Procurement of Medicines and Medical Consumables of the Public Medical Institutions in Tianjin (for trial implementation)* JYGBF〔2017〕No. 1	September 1, 2017
Qinghai	Partial implementation. From December 15, 2016 onwards, Two-invoice System is adopted for the varieties of medicines that have direct procurement and first-class agency for the drugs among successful bidding in the province, and the original delivery enterprises remain unchanged. Public medical institutions at all levels shall also give priority to the selection of medical consumables manufacturers and distribution enterprises that can adopt direct procurement and first-class agency, and gradually increase distribution concentration	*Implementation Opinions on the Two-invoice System to Be Adopted in the Drug Procurement of the Public Medical Institutions in Qinghai Province (for trial implementation)* *Notice on the Relevant Matters of the Two-invoice System to Be Adopted in the Purchase and Sales of Medicines and Medical Consumables*	No clear timetable

续表

地区	对“两票制”的态度	公文号 / 名称	全面执行日
江苏泰州	泰州市所有公立医疗机构的普通耗材实行“两票制”。配送商在遴选条件：近3年无重大违法经营行为记录；在泰州市设有300 m^2 以上的医械储备阴凉库；在泰州市设有公司，且年销售普通耗材金额在5000万元以上	《泰州市公立医疗卫生机构医用普通耗材采购配送管理办法》（征求意见稿）	未有明确时间表
江苏启东	加入三明耗材限价采购联盟，实行“两票制”	《药品耗材联合限价采购协议》	2017年5月
江苏南京	高值耗材实行“两票制”，采集并参考其他省份的中标价格	《南京地区医疗机构2017年高值医用耗材集中招标采购实施方案》	2017年8月

资料来源：各省市政府网站、联讯证券研究院。

表4　各地“两票制”实施情况

地区	实施情况
福建	药品已经全省执行“两票制”。2017年1月1日起，耗材执行“两票制”
安徽	要求自2016年11月1日起，在全省公立医疗机构药品采购中推行“两票制”
青海	要求自2016年12月15日起，全省公立医疗机构药品采购实行直采和“两票制”，基层医疗机构允许在“两票制”的基础上再开一次药品购销发票，逐步实行“两票制”
重庆	2016年12月31日起启动实施“两票制”，2017年5月31日前为过渡期
陕西	自2017年1月1日起，全省城市公立医疗机构药品耗材采购实行“两票制”，在确保基层药品供应保障基础上，县、镇、村医疗卫生机构适时推行“两票制”
上海	全市所有公立医疗机构药品采购全部实行“两票制”。自2017年7月1日起实施，到2017年年底全市所有公立医疗机构实现药品采购“两票制”

Continued

Region	Attitude to the Two-invoice System	File No./full name	Date of full implementation
Taizhou, Jiangsu	All public medical institutions in Taizhou implement the Two-invoice System for general consumables. conditions for the selection of distributors: no material violations of law in business records in the past three years; have cool warehouse of more than 300 square meters for storage of medical equipment in Taizhou; have a company in Taizhou, and the annual sales of general consumables exceed 50 million yuan	*Management Method of Purchase and Distribution of Common Medical Consumables in the Public Medical Institutions in Taizhou* (*draft*)	No clear timetable
Qidong, Jiangsu	Joined Sanming procurement of consumables at limited prices alliance, and implement the Two-invoice System	*Purchasing Agreement for Drugs and Medical Consumables at Joint Limited Price*	May, 2017
Nanjing, Jiangsu	The Two-invoice System is implemented for high-value consumables; collect and consult the prices of successful bids in other provinces	*Implementation Plan of the Centralized Procurement of High-value Medical Appliances by Means of Bidding of the Public Medical Institutions in the Nanjing Area in 2017*	August, 2017

Source: The provincial and municipal government websites and Lianxun Securities Research Institute.

Table 4 The Two-invoice System implementation in different regions

Region	Status of implementation
Fujian	The Two-invoice System has been implemented for drugs in the province. The Two-invoice System was implemented for consumables as from January 1, 2017
Anhui	It was required that the public medical institutions in the province implement the Two-invoice System for drug procurement on November 1, 2016
Qinghai	It was required that the public medical institutions in Qinghai province adopt the direct procurement and the Two-invoice System for drug procurement from December 15, 2016. The primary medical institutions were permitted to issue another invoice for purchase and sale of drugs under the Two-invoice System, thus enabling the Two-invoice System is to be gradually implemented
Chongqing	The Two-invoice System was launched on December 31, 2016. The transitional period lasts until May 31, 2017
Shaanxi	As from January 1, 2017, the public medical institutions in the province implement the Two-invoice System for purchase of pharmaceuticals and consumables, and, while ensuring the supply of drugs at the primary level, medical and health institutions at the county, township and village levels launch the Two-invoice System in due time
Shanghai	All public medical institutions in the city implement the Two-invoice System for purchase of drugs. It was implemented since July 1, 2017. All public health institutions in the city implemented the Two-invoice System for drug procurement by the end of 2017

续表

地区	实施情况
山西	2017年8月1日起，全省公立医疗机构采购药品全面实行“两票制”
辽宁	2017年6月1日起全省各级公立医疗机构启动实施药品采购“两票制”；2017年9月1日起全省各级公立医疗机构全面实施药品“两票制”
天津	2017年8月31日前为执行“两票制”过渡期；2017年9月1日起，全市公立医疗机构药品采购执行“两票制”
黑龙江	2017年8月31日前为过渡期；2017年9月1日起，正式全面实施“两票制”。全省所有公立医疗机构（含基层医疗机构，村卫生室药品由乡镇卫生院代购）药品采购全部实行“两票制”，鼓励其他医疗机构药品采购中推行“两票制”
广西	2017年9月1日起，自治区公立医院综合改革国家联系试点城市柳州、玉林、桂林、百色、防城港市率先实施“两票制”，鼓励其他医疗机构在药品采购中推行“两票制”。2017年9月1日前为过渡期；2018年1月1日起，其他所有设区市的公立医疗机构（包括基层医疗卫生机构）全面实行“两票制”，不另设过渡期
吉林	全省所有公立医疗机构药品采购全部实行“两票制”；全省自2017年6月30日起，正式实施“两票制”；暂定2017年9月30日后全部实行“两票制”
四川	从2017年4月6日起施行。给予5个月的过渡时间，允许药品生产、流通企业和公立医疗机构在过渡时间内消化库存、调整并重构药品供应链体系
湖南	自2017年4月12日起启动实施“两票制”，2017年9月30日前为过渡期。2017年10月1日起全省公立医疗机构正式全面实施“两票制”。全省所有公立医疗机构（含政府办基层医疗卫生机构，村卫生室药品可由乡镇卫生院代购）药品采购全面实行“两票制”，鼓励其他医疗机构药品采购实行“两票制”
甘肃	全省三级公立医院须于2017年10月1日起全面贯彻落实“两票制”
海南	2017年11月1日起，全省所有公立医疗机构全面实施“两票制”
河北	2017年11月1日前为过渡期
浙江	自2017年8月1日起实施，过渡期至2017年10月31日。全省公立医疗机构药品采购推行“两票制”
内蒙古	全区公立医疗机构（含基层医疗卫生机构）全部纳入“两票制”实施范围。2017年11月1日，全面实行“两票制”

Continued

Region	Status of implementation
Shanxi	Public medical institutions in the province fully implement the Two-invoice System for drug procurement as from August 1, 2017
Liaoning	From June 1, 2017, the Two-invoice System was launched by public medical institutions at all levels across the province. The Two-invoice System for drugs was fully implemented by public medical institutions at all levels in the province on September 1, 2017
Tianjin	The transitional period for the implementation of the Two-invoice System commenced on August 31, 2017. Since September 1, 2017, the public medical institutions in the city implement the Two-invoice System for drug procurement
Heilongjiang	The transitional period lasted until August 31, 2017. The Two-invoice System is fully implemented since September 1, 2017. All public medical institutions in the province (including primary medical institutions; the drugs for village clinics are procured by township hospitals) implement the Two-invoice System for drug procurement and other medical institutions are encouraged to implement the Two-invoice System for drug procurement
Guangxi	From September 1, 2017, the state liaison pilot cities for comprehensive medical reform including Liuzhou, Yulin, Guilin, Baise and Fangchenggang took the lead in the implementation of the Two-invoice System. Other medical institutions are encouraged to implement the Two-invoice System for drug procurement. The transitional period lasted until September 1, 2017. Since January 1, 2018, all other public medical institutions (including primary medical and health institutions) in the cities consisting of districts fully implement the Two-invoice System, without the transitional period
Jilin	All public medical institutions in the province implement the Two-invoice System for drug procurement. The Two-invoice System was officially implemented in the province on June 30, 2017. It is tentatively decided that the Two-invoice System is implemented fully on September 30, 2017
Sichuan	It comes into force as from April 6, 2017. There is a 5-month transitional period. Drug production and circulation enterprises and public health institutions digest inventories, and adjust and reorganize the pharmaceutical supply chain system during the transitional period
Hunan	The Two-invoice System was implemented on April 12, 2017, and the transitional period lasted until September 30, 2017. Public medical institutions in the province formally implemented the Two-invoice System fully on October 1, 2017. All public medical institutions in the province (including primary medical institutions; the drugs for village clinics are procured by township hospitals) implement the Two-invoice System for drug procurement and other medical institutions are encouraged to implement the Two-invoice System for drug procurement
Gansu	Tertiary public hospitals in the province must fully implement the Two-invoice System on October 1, 2017
Hainan	All public medical institutions in the province fully implemented the Two-invoice System on November 1, 2017
Hebei	The period before November 1, 2017 is the transitional period
Zhejiang	It came into force on August 1, 2017, and the period before October 31, 2017 is the transitional period. The public medical institutions in the province implement the Two-invoice System for drug procurement
Inner Mongolia	Public health institutions (including primary health care institutions) in the region are all included in the implementation scope of the Two-invoice System. The Two-invoice System was fully implemented on November 1, 2017

续表

地区	实施情况
湖北	全省所有公立医疗机构药品采购全部实行“两票制”。自2017年6月9日起实施，到2017年12月31日前为过渡期。2018年1月1日所有公立医疗机构全面实施“两票制”
江苏	全省各级公立医疗机构（含基层医疗卫生机构和村卫生室）。鼓励部队医院、民营医院、个体诊所等其他医疗机构在药品采购中积极推行“两票制”。与省采购同步执行“两票制”。第一批已上网采购的急（抢）救类、妇儿专科非专利等药品须于2017年12月31日前全面执行“两票制”
河南	全省公立医院综合改革试点城市要在2017年年底全面执行“两票制”；其他地区要在2018年6月底前全面执行“两票制”
山东	2017年11月1日起，济南、青岛、东营、潍坊、威海、滨州6个试点城市率先启动实施“两票制”；2017年12月31日起，全省各级公立医疗机构全面启动实施“两票制”
江西	全省公立医疗机构药品采购中逐步推行“两票制”。2017年，先行在公立医院改革试点城市推行“两票制”，到2018年在全省全面推开
广东	2017年12月2日起启动实施“两票制”，过渡期为6个月。2018年6月1日起全省所有公立医疗机构药品交易正式全面实施“两票制”

资料来源：各地政府公告，莫尼塔研究。

（七）各地执行“两票制”的相关信息汇总

表5是国家层面和31个省（区、市）“两票制”实施方案的部分重要信息按照实施方案规定的“两票制”的启动时间顺序排列的汇总比较。表5中有17个省市区明确地指出了“两票制”实施的主导部门，国家层面及14个省市区的“两票制”实施方案并未制定具体主导部门而是由卫生计生行政部门、中医药行政部门、食品药品监督管理部门、商务部门、税务部门、公安部门等多部门参与。除国家层面的实施方案外，各省（区、市）的实施方案均明确规定了区域内“两票制”的实施进程，指出了区域内医改试点城市应率先实行“两票制”，争取在2018年1月1日前全部公立医疗机构实施“两票制”。

Continued

Region	Status of implementation
Hubei	All public medical institutions in the province implement Two-invoice System for drug procurement. It came into force on June 9, 2017; the period before December 31, 2017 is the transitional period. On January 1, 2018, all public medical institutions fully implemented the Two-invoice System
Jiangsu	Public medical institutions at all levels (including primary medical and health institutions and village clinics) implement the Two-invoice System. Other medical institutions including military hospitals, private hospitals, and individually owned clinics are encouraged to promote the Two-invoice System for drug procurement. The Two-invoice System was implemented in tandem with the provincial procurement. The Two-invoice System must be fully implemented for the first batch of generic drugs for emergency rescue and gynecology and pediatrics purposes for online purchase before December 31, 2017
Henan	Pilot cities for comprehensive reform of public hospitals in the province fully implemented the Two-invoice System at the end of 2017; other areas fully implemented the Two-invoice System by the end of June 2018
Shandong	Since November 1, 2017, six pilot cities of Jinan, Qingdao, Dongying, Weifang, Weihai and Binzhou take the lead in launching the implementation of the Two-invoice System. Since December 31, 2017, the public health institutions at all levels in the province fully launch the implementation of the Two-invoice System
Jiangxi	Public medical institutions in the province gradually implement the Two-invoice System for drug procurement. In 2017, the Two-invoice System was first promoted in pilot cities for the reform of public hospitals and it was fully implemented in the province in 2018
Guangdong	The Two-invoice System was launched on December 2, 2017, and there is a 6-month transitional period. All the public medical institutions in the province officially and fully implemented the Two-invoice System on June 1, 2018

Source: Local government announcements, and CEBM study.

(VII) Summary of the information of the implementation of the Two-invoice System in different regions

Table 5 is the summary and comparison of some important information on the Two-invoice System implementation plan at the national level and in 31 provinces (autonomous regions and municipalities) in the order of the launch time of the Two-invoice System as specified in the implementation plan. In Table 5, 17 provinces (autonomous regions and municipalities) clearly stipulates the leading department of the Two-invoice System implementation; for the Two-invoice System implementation plan at the national level and in 14 provinces (autonomous regions and municipalities), it is undertaken by many departments including the health and family planning administrative department, Chinese medicine administration department, food and drug supervision and administration department, commerce department, tax department, public security department and so on. Apart from the implementation plan at the national level, the implementation plans of all provinces (autonomous regions and municipalities) clearly stipulate the implementation process of the Two-invoice System in the jurisdiction. It is pointed out that the Two-invoice System shall first be implemented in the pilot cities for medical reform in the region, and all public health institutions shall endeavor to implement the Two-invoice System before January 1, 2018.

表 5　各地“两票制”实施方案的部分重要信息汇总比较

地区	发文字号	主导部门	启动时间	实施进程
全国	国医改办发〔2016〕4 号	多部门参与	2016 年 12 月 26 日	综合医改试点省（区、市）和公立医院改革试点城市要率先推行“两票制”，鼓励其他地区执行“两票制”，争取到 2018 年在全国全面推开
福建	闽食药监市〔2009〕340 号	福建省食品药品监督管理局	2009 年 10 月 1 日	2010 年 5 月，实施基药集中采购“两票制”；2012 年 3 月实施非基药集中采购“两票制”
安徽	皖食药监药化流〔2016〕37 号	安徽省食品药品监督管理局	2016 年 11 月 1 日	2016 年 11 月 1 日起，在全省公立医疗机构药品采购中推行“两票制”
重庆	渝卫药政发〔2016〕92 号	重庆市卫生计生委	2017 年 1 月 1 日	2017 年 5 月 31 日前为过渡期。2017 年 6 月 1 日起，全面实施
青海	青政办〔2016〕219 号	青海省卫生计生委	2016 年 12 月 15 日	2016 年 12 月 15 日起，对直采和一级代理的药品品种实行“两票制”。2017 年进一步推进
陕西	陕医改办发〔2016〕8 号	卫生计生行政部门	2017 年 1 月 1 日	2017 年 1 月 1 日起，全省城市公立医疗机构药品耗材采购实行“两票制”
山西	晋医改办发〔2017〕27 号	多部门参与	2017 年 5 月 1 日	2017 年 7 月 31 日前为过渡期。2017 年 8 月 1 日全面推行
宁夏	宁药招办发〔2017〕16 号	医疗机构药品器械统一招标采购领导小组	2017 年 6 月 1 日	2017 年 6—8 月为过渡期，2017 年 8 月起，新一轮公立医疗机构招标药品、国家和宁夏谈判药品、基础输液和国家定点生产药品实行“两票制”管理。2018 年 1 月起，公立医疗机构挂网药品实行“两票制”管理

Table 5 Summary and comparison of some important information on the implementation plan of the Two-invoice System in different regions

Region	Document No.	Leading department	Launch date	Implementation process
Nationwide	GYGBF〔2016〕No. 4	Participation of multiple departments	December 26, 2016	Pilot provinces (autonomous regions and municipalities) for comprehensive medical reform and pilot cities for the reform of public hospitals shall take the lead in implementing the Two-invoice System and other regions are encouraged to implement the Two-invoice System. Every effort is made to implement the system in China in 2018
Fujian	MSYJS〔2009〕No. 340	Fujian Food and Drug Administration	October 1, 2009	The Two-invoice System was implemented for the centralized procurement of essential drugs in May 2010. The Two-invoice System was implemented for the centralized procurement of non-essential drugs in March 2012
Anhui	WSYJYHL〔2016〕No. 37	Anhui Food and Drug Administration	November 1, 2016	The public medical institutions in the province implemented the Two-invoice System for drug procurement on November 1, 2016
Chongqing	YWYZF〔2016〕No. 92	Chongqing Municipal Health and Family Planning Commission	January 1, 2017	The period before May 31, 2017 is the transitional period. It was fully implemented on June 1, 2017
Qinghai	QZB〔2016〕No. 219	Qinghai Provincial Health and Family Planning Commission	December 15, 2016	Since December 15, 2016, the Two-invoice System was implemented for the drug varieties for direct procurement and first-level agency. It was further advanced in 2017
Shaanxi	SYGBF〔2016〕No. 8	Health and Family Planning Administration Department	January 1, 2017	On January 1, 2017, the urban public medical institutions in the province implemented the Two-invoice System for the procurement of drugs and consumables
Shanxi	JYGBF〔2017〕No. 27	Participation of multiple departments	May 1, 2017	The period before July 31, 2017 is the transitional period. It was fully implemented on August 1, 2017
Ningxia	NYZBF〔2017〕No. 16	Leading group for centralized bidding and procurement of drugs and instruments by medical institutions	June 1, 2017	The period from June to August of 2017 is the transitional period. Since August 2017, the Two-invoice System management was implemented for a new round of bidding for drugs by public medical institutions, negotiated drugs in the State and Ningxia, basic infusion and the drugs for designated state production. From January 2018, the public medical institutions implement the Two-invoice System management for drugs for online procurement

续表

地区	发文字号	主导部门	启动时间	实施进程
辽宁	辽卫发〔2017〕29 号	多部门参与	2017 年 6 月 1 日	2017 年 8 月 1 日前，生产企业确定配送关系。2017 年 9 月 11 日全面实施“两票制”
天津	津医改办发〔2017〕1 号	多部门参与	2017 年 6 月 1 日	过渡期为 3 个月。2017 年 9 月 1 日全面实施
黑龙江	黑卫规发〔2017〕13 号	卫生计生部门	2017 年 4 月 25 日	2017 年 8 月 31 日前为过渡期。2017 年 9 月 1 日起，正式全面实施“两票制”
广西	桂医改办〔2017〕18 号	医改办	2017 年 4 月 24 日	2017 年 9 月 1 日起，柳州、玉林、桂林、百色、防城港市率先实施,2017 年 9 月 1 日前为过渡期。2018 年 1 月 1 日，全面实施
四川	川卫发〔2017〕55 号	多部门参与	2017 年 4 月 6 日	5 个月的过渡期，2017 年 9 月全面实施
吉林	吉卫联发〔2017〕55 号	吉林省卫生计生委	2017 年 6 月 30 日	2017 年 9 月 30 日全面实施
湖南	湘医改办发〔2017〕1 号	湖南省卫生计生委	2017 年 4 月 1 日	2017 年 9 月 30 日前为过渡期。2017 年 10 月 1 日起全省全面实施
甘肃	甘医改办发〔2017〕12 号	多部门参与	2017 年 4 月 19 日	医改试点城市须按照本方案于 2017 年 6 月 30 日前率先推行“两票制”。全省三级公立医院 2017 年 10 月 1 日起全面贯彻落实“两票制”，二级公立医疗机构须于新一轮药品集中采购中标结果执行起全面落实“两票制”，2018 年年底前落实到位

Continued

Region	Document No.	Leading department	Launch date	Implementation process
Liaoning	LWF〔2017〕No. 29	Participation of multiple departments	June 1, 2017	The manufacturer determined the distribution relationship before August 1, 2017. The Two-invoice System was fully implemented on September 11, 2017
Tianjin	JYGBF〔2017〕No. 1	Participation of multiple departments	June 1, 2017	The transitional period is 3 months. It was fully implemented on September 1, 2017
Heilongjiang	HWGF〔2017〕No. 13	Health and Family Planning Department	April 25, 2017	The period before August 31, 2017 is the transitional period. The Two-invoice System was fully implemented on September 1, 2017
Guangxi	GYGB〔2017〕No. 18	Medical Reform Office	April 24, 2017	As from September 1, 2017, Liuzhou, Yulin, Guilin, Baise and Fangchenggang took the lead in the implementation and the period before September 1, 2017 is the transitional period. It was fully implemented on January 1, 2018
Sichuan	CWF〔2017〕No. 55	Participation of multiple departments	April 6, 2017	There is a 5-month transitional period. It was fully implemented in September, 2017
Jilin	JWLF〔2017〕No. 55	Jilin Health and Family Planning Commission	June 30, 2017	It was implemented on September 30, 2017
Hunan	XYGBF〔2017〕No. 1	Hunan Health and Family Planning Commission	April 1, 2017	The period before September 30, 2017 is the transitional period. It was fully implemented in the province on October 1, 2017
Gansu	GYGBF〔2017〕No. 12	Participation of multiple departments	April 19, 2017	The pilot cities for medical reform were required to take the lead in implementing the Two-invoice System before June 30, 2017 in accordance with the plan. Tertiary public hospitals in the province fully implemented the Two-invoice System on October 1, 2017. Second-level public medical institutions shall fully implement the Two-invoice System as from the execution of successful bid results for a new ground of the centralized procurement of drugs. It was put in place at the end of 2018

续表

地区	发文字号	主导部门	启动时间	实施进程
云南	云卫药政发〔2017〕2号	多部门参与	2017年10月1日	2017年10月1日，省级公立医院以及医改试点城市率先实行“两票制”，2018年4月1日，医改试点城市全部实施。2018年10月1日，全省全面实施
海南	琼医改办〔2017〕9号	海南省卫生计生委	2017年4月1日	2017年9月30日前为过渡期。2017年11月1日起，全省所有公立医疗机构全面实施“两票制”
河北	冀医改办〔2017〕2号	多部门参与	2017年5月23日	2017年11月1日前为过渡期。2017年11月1日正式实施
浙江	浙卫发〔2017〕47号	多部门参与	2017年8月1日	过渡期至2017年10月31日
内蒙古	内卫计规范〔2017〕5号	多部门参与	2017年7月1日	4个月的过渡期，2017年11月1日，全面实行“两票制”
山东	鲁卫发〔2017〕31号	卫生计生行政部门	2017年10月13日	过渡期6个月，2017年11月1日，医改试点城市率先实行“两票制”，2017年12月31日起，全省全面实施
上海	沪人社医〔2017〕246号	多部门参与	2017年6月30日	2017年年底全市全面实施
河南	豫医改办〔2017〕1号	各级卫生计生部门	2017年8月18日	2017年年底前，洛阳、焦作、濮阳、鹤壁、漯河、三门峡等6个公立医院综合改革试点城市所有公立医疗机构实行“两票制”。2018年6月底前，全省全面实施
北京	京医改办〔2017〕5号	多部门参与	2017年11月20日	过渡期3个月

Continued

Region	Document No.	Leading department	Launch date	Implementation process
Yunnan	YWYZF〔2017〕No. 2	Participation of multiple departments	October 1, 2017	On October 1, 2017, the provincial-level public hospitals and pilot cities for medical reform took the lead in implementing the Two-invoice System; on April 1, 2018, it was implemented in pilot cities for medical reform. It was fully implemented in the province on October 1, 2018
Hainan	QYGB〔2017〕No. 9	Hainan Health and Family Planning Commission	April 1, 2017	The period before September 30, 2017 is the transitional period. From November 1, 2017, all public medical institutions in the province fully implement the Two-invoice System
Hebei	JYGB〔2017〕No. 2	Participation of multiple departments	May 23, 2017	The period before November 1, 2017 is the transitional period. It was formally implemented on November 1, 2017
Zhejiang	ZWF〔2017〕No. 47	Participation of multiple departments	August 1, 2017	The transitional period lasted until October 31, 2017
Inner Mongolia	NWJGF〔2017〕No. 5	Participation of multiple departments	July 1, 2017	There is a 4-month transitional period. The Two-invoice System was fully implemented on November 1, 2017
Shandong	LWF〔2017〕No. 31	Health and Family Planning Administrative Department	October 13, 2017	There is a 6-month transitional period. On November 1, 2017, the pilot cities for medical reform took the lead in implementing the Two-invoice System. It was fully implemented on December 31, 2017
Shanghai	HRSY〔2017〕No. 246	Participation of multiple departments	June 30, 2017	It was fully implemented in the city at the end of 2017
Henan	YYGB〔2017〕No. 1	Health and Family Planning Departments at all levels	August 18, 2017	Before the end of 2017, all public medical institutions in the six pilot cities for comprehensive reform of public hospitals including Luoyang, Jiaozuo, Puyang, Hebi, Luohe and Sanmenxia implemented the Two-invoice System. By the end of June 2018, it would have been fully implemented in the province
Beijing	JYGB〔2017〕No. 5	Participation of multiple departments	November 20, 2017	The transitional period is 3 months

续表

地区	发文字号	主导部门	启动时间	实施进程
湖北	鄂医改办发〔2017〕2号	多部门参与	2017年6月1日	2017年12月31日前为过渡期，2018年1月1日，全省公立医疗机构正式全面实施“两票制”
广东	粤人设规〔2017〕11号	广东省省人力资源社会保障厅	2017年12月2日	过渡期6个月
新疆	新政办发〔2017〕66号	自治区网上药品集中采购工作领导小组	2017年4月25日	试点城市2017年年底前实施，2018年全区推行
西藏	藏卫发〔2017〕317号	区发改委（医改办、物价局）	2017年10月1日	医改试点城市2017年年底前推行，2018年1月1日前全区实施
江苏	苏医改办发〔2017〕12号	多部门参与	2017年4月13日	第二批竞价采购、议价采购、限价挂网采购药品自采购结果执行之日起同步执行“两票制”。第一批已上网采购的急（抢）救类、妇儿专科非专利等药品须于2017年12月31日前全面执行“两票制”
贵州	黔卫计发〔2017〕18号	多部门参与	2017年4月28日	执行时间最迟不得超过省级新一轮药品集中招标采购目录执行时间
江西	赣卫药政字〔2017〕8号	省深化医药卫生体制改革领导小组	2017年4月14日	2017年，先行在公立医院改革试点城市推行“两票制”，争取到2018年在全省全面推开

表6是全国32套“两票制”实施方案部分重要信息的汇总。

Continued

Region	Document No.	Leading department	Launch date	Implementation process
Hubei	EYGBF〔2017〕No. 2	Participation of multiple departments	June 1, 2017	The period before December 31, 2017 is the transitional period. Public medical institutions in the province officially implemented the Two-invoice System fully on January 1, 2018
Guangdong	YRSG〔2017〕No. 11	Human Resources and Social Security Department of Guangdong Province	December 2, 2017	There is a 6-month transitional period
Xinjiang	XZBF〔2017〕No. 66	Leading group for the centralized procurement of drugs for online purchase in the autonomous region	April 25, 2017	It was implemented in pilot cities before the end of 2017, and was promoted in 2018 throughout the region
Tibet	ZWF〔2017〕No. 317	Development and Reform Commission of the autonomous region (Medical Reform Office, Price Bureau)	October 1, 2017	It was implemented in pilot cities before the end of 2017, and was promoted in 2018 throughout the region
Jiangsu	SYGBF〔2017〕No. 12	Participation of multiple departments	April 13, 2017	The Two-invoice System is implemented simultaneously for the second batch of bidding procurement, negotiated procurement, and drug procurement for online bidding within limited price range as from the date of execution of procurement results. The Two-invoice System must be fully implemented for the first batch of generic drugs for emergency rescue and gynecology and pediatrics purposes for online purchase before December 31, 2017
Guizhou	QWJF〔2017〕No. 18	Participation of multiple departments	April 28, 2017	The execution time shall not be later than the execution time for the catalogue of a new round of centralized bidding procurement for drugs in the province
Jiangxi	GWYZZ〔2017〕No. 8	Leading Team of Deepening the Reform of Medical and Health System of Jiangxi Province	April 14, 2017	In 2017, the Two-invoice System was implemented in the pilot city of the reform of public hospitals. Every effort was made to promote the system in the province by 2018

Table 6 is the summary of important information on the 32 implementation plans of the Two-invoice System in the country.

表6　各地“两票制”实施方案部门信息汇总

	境外药品国内总代理视同生产企业	偏远加一票	与耗材“两票制”同步	与集中采购相结合
数量	32	25	3	30
地区简称	国、闽、皖、渝、青、陕、晋、宁、辽、津、黑、桂、川、吉、湘、甘、琼、冀、浙、内蒙古、鲁、沪、豫、京、鄂、粤、新、藏、苏、黔、赣、云	国、皖、渝、青、晋、宁、黑、桂、川、吉、湘、甘、云、琼、浙、内蒙古、沪、豫、鄂、粤、新、藏、苏、黔、赣	闽、青、陕	国、闽、皖、渝、青、晋、宁、辽、津、黑、桂、川、吉、云、湘、甘、琼、冀、浙、内蒙古、沪、豫、京、鄂、粤、新、藏、苏、黔、赣

（八）各地出台的“两票制”执行方案的异同点

（1）各省（区、市）“两票制”文件均要求公立医疗机构执行“两票制”大原则，大部分省（区、市）都考虑到偏远乡镇配送实际困难，允许多开一票。差异在于多开一票执行松紧程度，部分省市要求确需增加一票的偏远乡镇需先备案，或者需要对配送企业进行遴选。

（2）部分省（区、市）在执行“两票制”过程中，同时强调配送商的遴选，例如，福建和陕西限定配送商数量，福建省基药配送集中到10个配送商，非基药11家；陕西三级医院配送商不超过15家，二级医院药品配送商不超过5家、器械配送商不超过15家等。遴选条件多样化，如限定下限注册资本、在本省（区、市）有多大容积仓储、历史配送诚信记录等。

（3）境外药品国内总代理视同生产企业基本全国一致，境内药品国内总代理是否认同工业一票有差异。目前，仅广西、海南认同境内药品国内总代理视同一票，宁夏规定省总代理也可视为工业，更宽松，但期限只到2017年年底。

Table 6 Summary of the information on the departments for the implementation plan of the Two-invoice System in different regions

	Domestic general agent of overseas pharmaceuticals deemed as manufacturers	An additional invoice for remote areas	Synchronized with the Two-invoice System for consumables	Combined with the centralized procurement
Quantity	32	25	3	30
Abbreviation of regions	State, Fujian, Anhui, Chongqing, Qinghai, Shaanxi, Shanxi, Ningxia, Liaoning, Tianjin, Heilongjiang, Guangxi, Sichuan, Jilin, Hunan, Gansu, Hainan, Hebei, Zhejiang, Inner Mongolia, Shandong, Shanghai, Henan, Beijing, Hubei, Guangdong, Xinjiang, Tibet, Jiangsu, Guizhou, Jiangxi, Yunnan	State, Anhui, Chongqing, Qinghai, Shanxi, Ningxia, Heilongjiang, Guangxi, Sichuan, Jilin, Hunan, Gansu, Yunnan, Hainan, Zhejiang, Inner Mongolia, Shanghai, Henan, Hubei, Guangdong, Xinjiang, Tibet, Jiangsu, Guizhou, Jiangxi	Fujian, Qinghai, Shaanxi	State, Fujian, Anhui, Chongqing, Qinghai, Shanxi, Ningxia, Liaoning, Tianjin, Heilongjiang, Guangxi, Sichuan, Jilin, Yunnan, Hunan, Gansu, Hainan, Hebei, Zhejiang, Inner Mongolia, Shanghai, Henan, Beijing, Hubei, Guangdong, Xinjiang, Tibet, Jiangsu, Guizhou, Jiangxi

(VIII) Similarities and differences among the implementation plans of the Two-invoice System issued by different regions

(1) Two-invoice System documents in all provinces (autonomous regions and municipalities) require the public medical institutions to implement the Two-invoice System principle. Most provinces (autonomous regions and municipalities) allow an additional invoice in view of the actual difficulties in the distribution to remote villages and towns. The difference lies in the degree of enforceability for the additional invoice. Some provinces (autonomous regions and municipalities) require the remote villages and towns requiring an additional invoice to file for the record first, or select the delivery enterprises.

(2) In the implementation of the Two-invoice System, some provinces (autonomous regions and municipalities) also emphasize the selection of distributors. For instance, Fujian and Shaanxi limit the number of distributors; in Fujian, there are 10 distributors of essential drugs and 11 for non-essential drugs; in Shaanxi, not more than 15 for tertiary hospitals, not more than 5 for secondary hospitals for drugs, and not more than 15 for medical instruments. There are diverse selection criteria, such as the minimum registered capital, storage capacity in the province (autonomous region or municipality), records of previous distribution and so on.

(3) Domestic general agent of overseas pharmaceuticals deemed as manufacturer is basically the same nationwide. There is difference on whether the domestic general agent of domestic pharmaceuticals agrees with the industrial invoice. At present, only Guangxi and Hainan accept the domestic general agent of domestic pharmaceuticals as one invoice. Regulations in Ningxia stipulate that the provincial general agent can also be regarded as industrial and the rules are more relaxed, but

（4）各省（区、市）“两票制”政策均列明“例外”品种可不执行“两票制”。如麻醉药品、第一类精神药品、计划生育药品、计划免疫药品（疫苗）、中药饮片等。

（5）大多数省（区、市）目前仅针对药品购销实施“两票制”，部分省（区、市）“两票制”政策涵盖器械耗材领域，如福建、陕西、天津及江苏部分地市(泰州、启东、南京)。

the deadline expired at the end of 2017.

(4) Two-invoice System policies in different regions list “exception” varieties that are inapplicable to the Two-invoice System, such as narcotic drugs, psychotropic substances in category Ⅰ, family planning drugs, planned immunization drugs, Chinese medicine decoction pieces and so on.

(5) Most provinces (autonomous regions and municipalities) currently implement the Two-invoice System only for drug purchases and sales. Some provinces (autonomous regions and municipalities) have Two-invoice System policies covering equipment consumables, such as Fujian, Shaanxi, Tianjin and parts of Jiangsu (Taizhou, Qidong and Nanjing).

七、药品购销“两票制”政策对医药行业的影响

（一）传统模式下，制药企业的渠道管理取决于它们的销售模式

1. 自营销售模式

自营销售模式即各地组建自己的销售公司或者销售团队来完成药品的开发，并进行临床推广活动，实现最终销售。大多数外资企业或国内一部分大型制药公司建立自有销售团队，因此，其部分业务中已经采用了“两票制”的渠道管理模式，特别是其主流市场，包括大型城市内的公立医疗机构和大型公立医院。但自有销售模式同时也会采用一些非“两票制”的经营模式，商务团队规模较小，药企委任大商业企业实现商业渠道管理外包；产品物流要求高费用，药企通过规模化物流和大商业企业调拨降低成本；部分终端医院或下级商业规模小型企业资金周转能力差，药企通过大商业的调拨提高回款速度。

2. 底价代理模式

底价代理模式即企业以底价现款供货给代理商，代理商控制渠道和终端实现最终销售。代理商通过商业过票或向厂家支付税金的方式解决收入和费用。国内大多数制药公司采用底价代理模式，其中包括各类大中小型制药企业。在“两票制”要求下，传统底价代理模式将被终结。在底价代理模式下，“过票商业”是其中的重要一环。在“两票制”改革前，部分采用“底价代理”模式的药品生产企业低价销售药品给代理商，经过多环节经销，最终将药品高价销售给终端医疗机构。通过层层“过票”后最终将差价返还给生产企业。在这种方式下，药企的外部经销商可以获得必要的费用支持来进行相关销售工作。

然而，在“两票制”政策环境下，底价代理模式的制药企业不仅需要重构其销售模式，同时也因为渠道管理权的转移而必须重构其渠道管理工作。

（二）对药品工业企业的影响

为了应对药品出厂价格被披露而引起物价部门对极高流通利润率的质疑，药品生

VII. The impact of the Two-invoice System policy in the purchase and sales of drugs on the pharmaceutical industry

(I) Under the traditional model, the channel management of pharmaceutical companies depends on their sales model

1. Self-sale model

In other words, this model is that each region sets up their own sales company or sales team to complete the development of drugs, and carry out clinical promotion activities to achieve the final sale. Most foreign-funded enterprises or some large Chinese pharmaceutical companies have established their own sales teams. Therefore, Two-invoice System channel management mode has been adopted in some of their businesses, especially in their mainstream markets including public medical institutions in large cities and large-scale public hospitals. However, the self-sale model also adopts some non-Two-invoice System business model. The business team has small scale, so pharmaceutical companies entrust large commercial enterprises to achieve the commercial channel outsourcing management. Since logistics of products require high costs, pharmaceutical enterprises reduce costs through large-scale logistics and extensive commercial allocation. Some terminal hospitals or small enterprises at a lower level have poor liquidity, so pharmaceutical companies improve the speed of payment through the allocation of large businesses.

2. Agency model at the floor price

In this model, the company supplies goods to the agent at the floor price in cash, and the agent controls the channel and the terminal to achieve the final sale. Agents solve the issue of income and costs through the improper use of invoice or paying taxes to the manufacturers. Most domestic pharmaceutical companies use the agency model at the floor price, including all types of small, medium and large pharmaceutical companies. Under the Two-invoice System, the traditional agency model at the floor price will be abolished. Under the agency model at the floor price, "the business featuring the improper use of invoice issued by the pharmaceutical enterprise" is an important part of it. Before the Two-invoice System reform, some drug manufacturers that adopted the "agency model at the floor price" sold drugs to agents at low prices, and the drugs were eventually sold to terminal medical institutions at a high price via many links. Through the links of "improper use of invoice", the final price difference was returned to the manufacturer. In this way, the external distributors of pharmaceutical enterprises can obtain the necessary cost support to carry out the sales.

However, under the Two-invoice System policy, the pharmaceutical companies adopting the agency model at the floor price not only restructure their sales model, but also reorganize their channel management due to the transfer of channel management rights.

(II) Impact on the pharmaceutical industry enterprises

In order to dispel the doubts of the price department about the extremely high distribution profit rate due to the disclosure of the ex-factory prices of pharmaceutical products, pharmaceutical

产企业提高药品出厂价格，直接开票给实际配送流通企业，由药品生产企业承担“走票”的法律和税务风险，不再允许流通企业“走票”。高开的药品出厂价包含生产成本和大部分销售费用（包括给医院和医师的“回扣”）。而高开的出厂价税票主要是通过虚开原料、包材、餐饮、差旅、广告宣传、交通、会务等费用发票来冲账，再洗出现金返利给各利益相关方。这种方式主要存在于大型制药企业或科工贸一体化的集团型企业，被称为直营制的“高开高返”模式。在该模式下，药品从生产企业到流通企业开一次发票，从流通企业到医疗卫生机构开一次发票，药品流通过程基本可实现“两票”，然而其通过“走票”方式偷逃税款的本质仍未改变。

但随着“营改增”的全面推广和税务系统的升级，各种其他行业能够提供的冲账税票将会越来越难获得，制药企业的“走票”漏洞将被逐渐封堵。加上“两票制”政策实施下，相关部门的监管压力和成本大幅下降，监管强度加大，药品生产企业“走票”的难度和风险将越来越高。因此，如何应对激涨的税务负担将会是所有药品生产企业在该政策实施下面临的首要难题。“两票制”对药品生产企业的影响如图 7 所示。

共性问题	个性问题（MNC）	个性问题（内资企业）
·业务扁平化、成本增加 ·回款机制缺失、代理商的垫资功能弱化 ·财税方式变化引起营销模式变化 ·工业企业成为责任和风险主体 ·产品终端价格及渠道控制	·运营模式调整（区分专利药、过期专利药；进口渠道与原研地产化产品间的协调；转授权；联合开发；MAH） ·分销方式调整（进口商数量、一级代理） ·推广方式调整（自营、外包 CSO、过专利期药的所有权转移）	·自营方式升级与完善 ·渠道优化 ·推广优化 ·财税合规 ·放弃底价模式 ·渠道重构 ·财税方式重构 ·推广方式重构 ·财税合规

图 7　“两票制”对药品生产企业的影响

manufacturing enterprises increase the ex-factory prices of medicines and directly issue invoice to the actual delivery and circulation enterprises, and pharmaceutical manufacturing enterprises bear the legal and tax risks of "the business of an intermediary which engages in the business of medicines despite of its lack of relevant qualification". Circulation enterprises are not allowed to engage in the business of an intermediary which engages in the business of medicines despite of its lack of relevant qualification. The high ex-factory prices of medicines include the cost of production and most of the selling expenses (including "rebates" to hospitals and physicians). The high ex-factory price tax is mainly canceled by the false invoices of fees including raw materials, packaging materials, catering, travel, advertising, transportation, and conference. The illegally obtained cash is returned to various stakeholders. This approach is mainly adopted by large-scale pharmaceutical enterprises or group enterprises integrating R&D, production and marketing. It is known as the "high invoicing amount and high return" mode under the self-sale system. Under this model, the drug distribution process basically results in the Two-invoice System when one invoice is issued for drugs from the manufacturing enterprise to the circulation enterprise, and another issued for drugs from the circulation enterprise to the medical and health institutions. However, the nature of tax evasion through "the business of an intermediary which engages in the business of medicines despite its lack of relevant qualification" remains unchanged.

However, with the overall promotion of the Business Tax Replaced with Value-added Tax and the upgrade of the tax system, it is increasingly difficult for various other industries to provide tax receipts for reversing entries. The loopholes of the "business of the pharmaceutical companies of an intermediary which engages in the business of medicine despite of its lack of relevant qualification" by pharmaceutical enterprises will be gradually closed. Coupled with the implementation of the Two-invoice System policy, the pressure regulatory oversight and significant cost reduction, there are higher difficulty and risks of "business of an intermediary which engages in the business of medicines despite of its lack of relevant qualification" for pharmaceutical manufacturers. Therefore, how to cope with the soaring tax burden will be the primary challenge that all drug manufacturers face in the implementation of this policy. The impact of the Two-invoice System on pharmaceutical manufacturers is shown in Figure 7.

Common problems	Individuality problems (MNC)	Individuality problems (domestic-funded enterprises)
· Flat business and cost increase · Lack of fund recovery mechanism and weakened function of advance payment by agents · Change in finance and tax modes leading to change in marketing model · Industrial enterprises become the principal parts of responsibility and risks · Terminal price of products and channel control	· Adjustment of operating model (differentiate the patent drugs and expired patent drugs; coordination of import channels and localized products of original drugs; sublicensing; joint development; MAH) · Adjustment of modes of distribution (number of importers; first-level agent) · Adjustment of modes of promotion (self-sale, contract sales organization, transfer of ownership of drugs after patent term)	· Upgrading and improving the mode of proprietary trading · Channel optimization · Promotion optimization · Finance and tax compliance · Waiver of floor price model · Channel reorganization · Reorganization of finance and tax modes · Reorganization of promotion methods · Finance and tax compliance

Figure 7　Impact of the Two-invoice System on pharmaceutical manufacturers

制药企业受到的影响主要有以下几项。

1. 取消调拨模式

取消调拨的同时，企业也丧失了调拨模式为业务带来的益处。需要大幅扩张商务团队直接管理所有经销商和终端，当一级商不再提供管理二级商的作用和义务，没有了一级商的垫资作用，在商业环境较差的地区中回款明显受公司内控政策要求影响，部分“必需经销商”却因资信等问题难以发展为一级商业企业。

2. 成本费用增加

特殊产品（如冷链）的物流配送规模效应降低，物流成本费用增加；缺少“人脉更熟”的当地商业配合，与当地小型商业沟通的业务成本将增大；商业合作模式出现障碍；药厂之间的商业合作，如药品许可协议、部分区域产品权益转让等各种合作模式因“两票制”环境下企业之间开票受限而无法开展。

3. 客户管理难度上升

此前药企只要统管几个一级代理商（流通商）即可，销售系统级层下面二级、三级甚至基层代理 / 流通商由相应上级代理商管理，客户管理难度较小；“两票制”后，出于压缩流通环节需要，所有二级、三级代理 / 流通商都升级为一级代理商，销售系统虽然扁平化，但是对药企来说，将面对管理众多一级客户的难度。营销管理难度加大，因一级配送商业数量大大增加，渠道管理难度也随之加大；混合模式并存，同一区域不同代理人共用配送商业；企业代替原先居间人直接管理渠道，需要重构或加强渠道管理能力。

4. 渠道调整，业绩增速短期受影响

全国“两票制”的逐步落地执行，尤其是部分省（区、市）在执行“两票制”过程中限制流通配送商数量，遴选配送商名单，导致医药商业向大型商业企业集中，中小代理商退出，清理渠道库存，部分企业业绩增速短期受影响。由于缺乏市场和销售推广费用，此类产品需要“广种薄收”的市场覆盖，对商业公司的渠道覆盖能力要求很高，没有原先“过票公司”的垫资作用，存在一定资金压力，需要重构或加强渠道管理能力。企业、经销商 / 居间人和商业公司之间的关系发生明显变化，经销商对产品的掌控能力可能下降，对销售存在一定不利影响。

Pharmaceutical companies are chiefly affected by the following aspects.

1. Cancellation of the allocation mode

While the allocation is canceled, the enterprises also lose the benefit brought by the allocation model for the business. The business team shall be significantly expanded to directly manage all dealers and terminals. When the first-level dealer no longer has the role and obligation to manage the second-level dealers, and there is no advance payment by first-level dealers, the recovery of fund is significantly affected by the internal control policies of enterprise in the areas with poor business climate. Some "essential dealers" have difficulty in developing into first-level commercial enterprises due to credit and other issues.

2. Increase of costs

Since the economies of scale of logistics and distribution of special products (such as cold chains) is reduced, logistics costs increase; there is a lack of cooperation with local businesses with "better connections", so costs of communication with local small businesses and business will increase; business cooperation mode faces obstacles; business cooperation between pharmaceutical enterprises, such as drug license agreement and transfer of product rights in some regions, cannot be carried out due to the limitation of invoicing among enterprises under the Two-invoice System environment.

3. The increasing difficulties in customer management

Previously pharmaceutical companies only exercise unified management of several first-level dealers (distributors), and agents/distributors at the second and third levels and even at primary level are managed by the superior dealers, with less difficulties in customer management; after the implementation of the Two-invoice System, all agents/distributors at the second and third levels are upgraded to first-level agents due to the needs of fewer circulation links. Although the sales system is flat, the pharmaceutical companies will face the difficulty of managing a large number of first-level customers. Marketing management becomes more difficult. As the first-level distribution businesses increase greatly, channel management becomes more difficult accordingly; there are mixed models, and different agents in the same region share the same distribution business; enterprises replace the original intermediary to directly manage the channels, and need to reconstruct or strengthen channel management capabilities.

4. Channel adjustment, and the impact on short-term performance growth

The Two-invoice System has been implemented in the country step by step. In particular, some provinces (autonomous regions and municipalities) restrict the number of distributors in the implementation of the Two-invoice System, and select the list of distributors, leading to the concentration of pharmaceutical enterprises to large enterprises, while small and medium-sized agents exit. Inventory of the channels is cleaned up, and the performance growth of some enterprises is affected in the short term. Due to the lack of marketing and sales promotion expenses, such products achieve market coverage through "extensive cultivation", and there are very high requirements for the channel coverage ability of commercial companies. Without the advance payment role of the "companies with business featuring the improper use of invoice issued by the pharmaceutical enterprise", there is some financial stress and they need to reorganize or strengthen channel management capabilities. Significant changes have taken place in the relationship among the company,

5. 纳税上升

在多级经销商销售模式中，大部分药品生产企业采用底价的低开销售模式，不承担出厂价和医疗机构终端价的差价部分的纳税义务。同时在“两票制”和“营改增”的双重打击下，通过层层经销商“过票”“挂票”等方式为高额代理费、劳务费甚至开方扣点等灰色费用提现的现象，不能再为一些违规企业获取利润。

6. 销售成本增加

商务管理成本增加；呆死账成本增加；由于缺乏一定的临床销售费用，产品销售额和销售价格均可能出现明显滑坡，制药企业需要承担所有药品费用和其中可能的风险；终端物流成本及回款风险可能因配送企业的增加和市场复杂性增加而增大。

7. 商业回款周期变化

传统模式下，配送商数量多，为争夺配送权，回款时间在短期内可能缩短；后期在“两票制”下，配送商的数量遭到限制，在有限的配送商之间，少量的配送商逐渐占据市场垄断地位，可能会出现“店大欺客”的现象，导致商业回款周期延长。

商务部发布的《2014 年药品流通行业运行统计分析报告》显示，2014 年，我国 179 家药品批发企业对医疗卫生机构平均应收账款周转天数为 122 天，应收账款总额高达 587.07 亿元，占对公立医疗卫生机构销售总额的 37.6%。个别医疗卫生机构在 6 个月回款期到期时选择给企业开具银行承兑汇票（通常承兑期为半年），将支付药品货款的时间又延长了 6 个月，而这也制约了药品流通企业流通及运营效率的提高。虽然《国务院办公厅关于完善公立医院药品集中采购工作的指导意见》(国办发〔2015〕7 号)明确指出，医疗卫生机构从交货验收合格到付款不得超过 30 天，然而在执行时，医疗卫生机构凭借其在药品供应链上的绝对强势地位，在无相应监管和惩戒制度的情况下，其财务部门往往不积极付款甚至有意拖欠货款，以致不能在 30 天内完成回款。究其原因，拖欠货款事实上也是医院获取返利的另一种体现形式。以 2014 年医院 587.07 亿元的拖欠款为例，仅按照 2014 年各银行半年定期存款利率的 2.80%～3.08% 计算，仅半年时间医院就有高达 8 亿～18 亿的利息收益。而在药品流通领域中，现金流是企业正常周转的生命线，企业在医院回款前，通常依靠“走票”洗出现金或向银行贷款维持生存。在“两票制”政策实施以后，通过“走票”洗出现金的渠道逐渐

the distributor/intermediary and the commercial company. The dealer's ability to control the product may weaken and the sales may be adversely affected somewhat.

5. Tax increase

In the multi-level dealer sales model, most drug manufacturers adopt the sales model of low invoice price at the floor price, and do not assume the tax payment obligation for the difference between the ex-factory price and the end price of medical institutions. Under the double whammy of the Two-invoice System and the Business Tax Replaced with Value-added Tax, some enterprises cannot obtain illegal profit from the withdrawal of high-amount agency fees, labor costs and even invoicing-based deduction through the "business featuring the improper use of invoice issued by the pharmaceutical enterprise" and "business of an intermediary which engages in the business of medicines despite of its lack of relevant qualification".

6. Increase of sales costs

Business management costs increase; bad debt costs increase; due to the lack of certain clinical marketing costs, the product sales volume and sales prices are likely to decline significantly. Pharmaceutical companies need to bear all the costs of medicines and possible risks; the risk of terminal logistics costs and the recovery of costs may increase due to the increase of distribution enterprises and the increase of market complexity.

7. Cycle changes in the recovery of costs

There are many distributors in the traditional mode. In order to compete for distribution rights, the time of fund recovery may be shortened in the short term; under the Two-invoice System, the number of distributors is limited. Among the limited distributors, only a few distributors will gradually corner the market, resulting in the "big store bullying the customers", and the extension of the recovery cycle of fund.

The *Statistical Analysis Report of the Operation of the Drug Distribution Enterprises in 2014* released by the Ministry of Commerce shows that in 2014, the average number of days of the turnover of accounts receivables of the 179 pharmaceutical wholesale enterprises in China from medical and health institutions was 122 days, and the accounts receivable total 58.707 billion yuan, accounting for 37.6% of the total sales from public health institutions. Some medical and health institutions choose to issue banker's acceptance (usually with a period of six months) when the six-month payment period expires, and the time for payment of medicines is extended by another six months, which restricts the efficiency of distribution and operation of pharmaceutical circulation enterprises. Although the *Guiding Opinions of the State Council on the Improvement of the Centralized Purchase of Medicines of Public Medical Institutions* (GBF〔2015〕No. 7) clearly states that the period from delivery and acceptance to payment by medical and health institutions shall not exceed 30 days, however, by dint of its absolute superiority in the pharmaceutical supply chain, the financial departments of medical and health institutions often fail to make timely payment or even intentionally fall into arrears in the absence of regulation or punishment system, resulting in the failure of collection of fund within 30 days. The late payment is actually another way for hospitals to receive rebates. For example, if a hospital falls into arrears with 58.707 billion yuan in 2014, the hospital can receive interest income of up to 0.8 billion to 1.8 billion yuan in six months based on the interest rate of 2.80%~3.08% for six-month fixed time deposit of the banks in 2014. In the field of drug circulation, cash flow is the lifeline of the normal

被封堵，若医院依旧严重占压批发企业资金，那么在税务负担激涨的情况下，还必须承担银行贷款高额财务负担，将极大地影响企业的正常运营，这是企业难以承受之重。因此，在整顿药品流通秩序过程中，应重视医院回款问题，建立促进医院及时回款的长效机制，落实医院回款具体负责人和相应惩戒措施，保障医药工商业的合法利益，使企业主动拥护政策的执行，为“两票制”政策的实施提供助力。

（三）对药品流通、配送及服务型企业的影响

1.“两票制”下对医药流通行业的影响

药品流通企业以基于市场竞争下的较低价格（仅包含生产成本和适当利润）从生产企业购进药品，再以高额差价销售给医院。其通过伪造多次转手的购销链条，购买增值税发票冲抵药品价格虚高部分，在偷逃增值税（17%）和所得税（25%）的同时获取现金，支付医药代表工资福利及医院和医师的灰色收入。这种方式在传统药品流通领域最为多见，被称作生产企业代理制的“低开高返”模式。“走票”行为成本低廉，药价在流通过程中增值幅度巨大，因此，大量小型药品流通企业仅依靠“走票”偷税、逃税即可基本实现营利，而这也是我国药品批发企业数量多达 13 000 余家，并且家家都可以存活的原因。而“两票制”政策剑指“低开高返”模式，在禁止药品多次转手的前提下，严格核查购销过程中的货、票信息，杜绝药品流通企业的“走票”行为。因此，大量依靠“走票”而生存的药品流通企业将在“两票制”政策实施进程中被清洗出局。

而随着“两票制”的推行可能会触发一轮新的流通洗牌。“两票制”逼迫所有医药商业公司巩固终端客户关系，终端客户的服务能力成为“两票制”政策下最核心要素。在“两票制”实施之前，商业调拨仍占据药品流通市场 41% 的比重，由此可以预期“两票制”的实施将对流通行业产生明显的洗牌效果。未来商业调拨销售主要体现为进口药品国内分销、针对零售和非公立医疗机构的市场调拨，以及“两票制”允许的对偏远基层市场的调拨第三票。

turnover of enterprises. Before the collection of fund from hospitals, enterprises often rely on "the business of an intermediary which engages in the business of medicine despite its lack of relevant qualification" to obtain cash or take out bank loans for survival. After the implementation of the Two-invoice System policy, the channel of obtaining cash through the "business of the pharmaceutical companies of an intermediary which engages in the business of medicine despite of its lack of relevant qualification" has been gradually closed. If the hospital still squeezes the funds of wholesaling enterprises, enterprises must bear the burden of high finance of bank loans under the soaring tax burden, which will greatly affect the normal operation of enterprises. This is unbearable for enterprises. Therefore, in the process of rectifying the order of circulation of medicines, attention shall be paid to the issue of payment by hospitals, the establishment of a long-term mechanism to promote timely payment by hospitals, and the implementation of measures for the specific person in charge of payments by hospitals and the corresponding disciplinary measures. As a result, this safeguards the legitimate interests of the pharmaceutical industry, enables the enterprises to support the implementation of the policy, and provides assistance for the implementation of the Two-invoice System policy.

(III) Impact on the pharmaceutical distribution, delivery and service-oriented enterprises

1. Impact on the pharmaceutical circulation industry under the Two-invoice System

Pharmaceutical distribution companies buy drugs from manufacturing enterprises at a low price based on the market competition (only including production costs and appropriate profits), and then sell the drugs to hospitals with high price difference. Pharmaceutical distribution companies falsify the purchase and sale chain through multiple transactions and buy value-added tax invoices to offset the falsely high portion of the price of medicines. They obtain cash to pay salary welfare for medical sales representatives and grey income for hospitals and physicians while evading value-added tax (17%) and income tax (25%). This method is the most common in the field of traditional medicine circulation and is called the "low invoicing amount and high rebate" mode of agency system of manufacturers. "Business of an intermediary which engages in the business of medicines despite of its lack of relevant qualification" entails low cost, and drug prices increase significantly in the process of circulation. Therefore, a large number of small drug circulation enterprises rely only on "business of an intermediary which engages in the business of medicines despite of its lack of relevant qualification" for tax evasion and can basically achieve profitability, which is why there are over 13 000 pharmaceutical wholesaling enterprises in China, and all these enterprises can survive. The policy of the Two-invoice System is unveiled to combat the "low invoicing amount and high rebate" mode. On the premise of banning the multiple transactions of drugs, the information of goods and invoice is verified during the purchase and sale process, eliminating the "business of an intermediary which engages in the business of medicines despite of its lack of relevant qualification" of drug circulation enterprises. Therefore, a large number of drug circulation enterprises that rely heavily on "business of an intermediary which engages in the business of medicines despite of its lack of relevant qualification" for survival will be eliminated during the implementation process of the Two-invoice System policy.

The Two-invoice System implementation may trigger a new round of circulation shuffle. The Two-invoice System impels all pharmaceutical commercial companies to consolidate their end-

针对主流的公立医院市场，医药商业公司将不得不缩减调拨业务，使得药品纯销市场的竞争核心转移到对公立医疗机构的掌控能力和市场份额争夺之中。

全国性大流通企业已经开始为“两票制”布局，主要通过渠道集中度提升和资金保障这两个环节入手。进口业务方面：大型龙头商业巨头已经开始为“两票制”布局，主要通过渠道集中度提升和资金保障这两个环节入手；集中采购业务方面：对于全国渠道布局良好的商业公司，其传统调拨业务可能转型为针对上游生产企业实施集中采购和增值服务及子公司获取重要品种的平台，从而加大市场机会和份额；资金保障方面：大型龙头商业企业具有多种融资渠道，为此能提供更强的资金保障能力，针对代理商 / 居间人转型过程中的资金周转问题，引入第三方金融保理服务；外延发展方面：优选具有终端配送能力的商业公司进行股权并购，夯实终端布局有利于对上游生产企业的议价能力和服务能力。

结合“零差价”“控增长”“控药占比”政策，未来商业调拨业务也很可能转化为零售服务业务，或是医院合作院边药房业务。从地域分布来看，“两票制”可能影响我国医药流通业布局，人口密度高和临床服务基础发达的终端区域将成为核心市场。“两票制”对市场增长影响有限，人口和医疗资源大省则孕育更多机遇。从福建省的“两票制”实践来看，福建当地的药品流通市场并未出现衰退。连续 6 年的市场复合增长率仅低于全国平均水平约 0.5%。据鹭燕医药招股说明书，福建省 2012 年 8 标药品配送商达 176 家，而据福建省药械集中采购网数据，2016 年配送商仅 40 家左右。除福建省指定的 药配送企业外，各片区增补配送商大多仅覆盖一个地市级片区，未来有望被现有龙头整合，配送集中度将进一步提升（表 7）。

customer relationships. The service ability of end customers is the most central element under the Two-invoice System policy. Prior to the implementation of the Two-invoice System, commercial allocation accounted for 41% of the pharmaceutical distribution market. Thus, it is expected that the implementation of the Two-invoice System will have a significant reshuffling effect on the circulation industry. In the future, commercial distribution sales will be mainly reflected in the domestic distribution of imported drugs, and the market allocation for retail and non-public medical institutions, as well as the allocation of third invoice for remote primary markets as permitted by the Two-invoice System.

For the mainstream public hospital market, the pharmaceutical commercial companies have to reduce the allocation business, and thus the core competition in the pharmaceutical direct-sale market shifts to the control of public medical institutions and the wrestle for market share.

The large circulation enterprises have begun to make layout for the Two-invoice System, mainly through the two channels, the channel concentration enhancement and capital guarantee. In terms of import business, large leading commercial giants have begun to make layout in the Two-invoice System mainly through two channels, the channel concentration enhancement and capital guarantee; in terms of centralized purchasing business, the commercial companies with established channels nationwide may transform the traditional allocation business into a platform for upstream manufacturing enterprises to implement centralized purchasing and value-added services as well as for subsidiaries to acquire important varieties, thereby increasing market opportunities and share. In terms of fund support, large leading commercial enterprises have various financing channels, so as to provide stronger financial guarantee capabilities for capital turnover during the transformation of agents/intermediaries, and introduce third-party financial factoring services; in terms of extended development, commercial companies with the terminal delivery capabilities are optimized for equity mergers and acquisitions. Consolidating the terminal layout is conducive to bargaining power and service capabilities with upstream manufacturers.

Coupled with the “zero price difference”, “control of growth” and “control of the proportion of the medicines which produce the operating revenue of a hospital”, the future commercial allocation business is also likely to be transformed into retail service business or business of pharmacy near hospitals. In terms of geographical distribution, the Two-invoice System may affect the layout of pharmaceutical distribution in China. The terminal area with a high population density and a well-developed clinical service base will become the core market. The Two-invoice System has had a limited impact on market growth, while major provinces with large population and rich medical resources have created more opportunities. From the viewpoint of the Two-invoice System practice in Fujian province, local drug market does not decline. For six straight years, the market compound growth rate is merely below the national average by about 0.5%. According to Prospectus of Luyan Pharmaceutical, there were 176 delivery companies for the 8th batch of drugs in 2012 in Fujian province. According to the data from the website of Fujian centralized procurement and sale of drugs and medical instruments, there were about 40 distributors in 2016. Except the pharmaceutical distribution enterprises designated by Fujian province, most of the additional distributors in each area only cover one prefecture-level area. In the future, it is expected to be integrated by the existing leaders and the distribution concentration will be enhanced (Table 7).

表 7　福建省覆盖 2 个及以上片区的 10 家配送商

配送企业	龙岩	南平	宁德	平潭	莆田	泉州	三明	厦门	省属（含福州）	漳州	片区数
国药控股福建 / 福州有限公司	✓	✓	✓	✓	✓	✓	✓	✓	✓	✓	10
鹭燕（福建）药业股份有限公司	✓	✓	✓		✓	✓	✓	✓	✓	✓	9
中邮恒泰药业有限公司	✓		✓	✓	✓	✓	✓		✓	✓	8
九州通医药有限公司				✓	✓		✓	✓	✓		5
惠好药业有限公司		✓			✓	✓	✓		✓		5
福建省医药有限责任公司		✓	✓	✓			✓		✓		5
厦门宏仁医药有限公司	✓							✓	✓	✓	4
福建同春药业股份有限公司	✓		✓				✓		✓		4
中鹭医药有限公司								✓	✓		2
泉州市东大医药有限责任公司						✓			✓		2

数据来源：福建药械集中采购网，鹭燕医药招股说明书，国泰君安证券研究报告。

Table 7 The 10 distributors that cover two areas and the above in Fujian province

Distribution companies	Longyan	Nanping	Ningde	Pingtan	Putian	Quanzhou	Sanming	Xiamen	Provincial-level (including Fuzhou)	Zhangzhou	Number of areas
Sinopharm Group Fujian / Fuzhou Co., Ltd.	√	√	√	√	√	√	√	√	√	√	10
Luyan (Fujian) Pharmaceutical Co., Ltd.	√	√	√		√	√	√	√	√	√	9
China Post Hengtai Pharmaceutical Co., Ltd.	√		√	√	√	√	√		√	√	8
Jointown Pharmaceutical Co., Ltd.				√	√		√	√	√		5
Huihao Pharmaceutical Co., Ltd.		√			√	√	√		√		5
Fujian Pharmaceutical Group Co., Ltd.		√	√	√			√		√		5
Xiamen Honest Medicine Co., Ltd.	√							√	√	√	4
Fujian Tongchun Pharmaceutical Co., Ltd.	√		√				√		√		4
Zhonglu Pharmaceutical Co., Ltd.								√	√		2
Quanzhou Dongda Pharmaceutical Co., Ltd.						√			√		2

Source: The website of Fujian centralized procurement and sale of drugs and medical instruments, Prospectus of Luyan Pharmaceutical, Guotai Jun'an Securities Research Report.

从福建省的“两票制”实践来看，三明医院端配送份额基本由3家瓜分：鹭燕医药、国控、惠民配送82%的品种，在第三终端鸿福一家独大（80%）。三明采购方案中明确配送费用包含在报价中，其中非基药配送费用按报价8%执行，基药、大输液配送费用按10%执行。三明市从医保资金中预付一个月的药品货款给药品配送企业，作为周转金，同时严格执行30天账期。

但是，在“两票制”下，流通企业要同时面临来自药品生产企业和终端医疗机构的财务压力。当面临账款无法及时收回的情况时，流通企业需面临垫收货款的压力，这无疑对流通企业是一个重大的考验。而一批只具有渠道推广能力，不具备配送能力的分销商将被淘汰，面临着转型问题。在行业整合的过程中，医药批发行业必将产生严峻的竞争态势。而在竞争压力下，医药流通公司只有通过经营上的规模化、产业化、专业化的发展，通过企业自身管理能力的提高和业务手段的转变，才能保证其在面临市场震荡和行业整合时不受到影响。

2. 对营销服务型企业的影响

在“两票制”下，中小型流通企业面临经营模式转型，从代理型商业调整为营销服务型企业。“两票制”和“营改增”新政压缩药品流通环节，行业走向规范化，提升行业集中度，以“过票”或“倒票”为主的批发企业将退出行业。传统的商业模式和财税处理模式已经无法适应新政下行业发展的要求，必须要重塑商业模式。拥有GSP的代理商，如果不能转型为配送商就只能转变为专业从事市场推广活动的市场服务商（CSO）。药品生产企业与CSO签订委托服务协议，按照协议内容支付对价。通过重塑新商业模式，药企与CSO建立合法合规的服务关系，降低药品流通领域的相关财税风险。对代理商而言，原来的一级和大规模区域代理商会继续拓展自己的渠道网络，提高覆盖率，并加强对终端资源的掌控；而二级及以下的代理商的未来转型有很多种可能，或通过与生产商谈判升级为一级代理商，或被一级代理商收购，成为其销售外包商，或者转型为配送商。在转型过程中，生产企业必须根据自身产品的特点、目标医院分布及成本等考量因素，合理选择代理商并建立新的合作关系；而代理商则根据自己的能力和未来发展规划，重新和生产商谈判划分渠道责任，以保证最大利益。

Judging from the Two-invoice System practice in Fujian province, the distribution share of Sanming hospital is basically shared by three companies: Luyan Pharmaceutical, Sinopharm Group, and Huimin Pharmaceutical—delivering 82% of the varieties. In the third terminal, Hongfu Pharmaceutical has the dominant position (80%). Sanming procurement program clearly stipulates that the distribution costs are included in the quote. Delivery costs of non-essential medicines are subject to 8% of the quote, and delivery costs of base drugs and infusion are subject to 10%. In Sanming, the payment of drugs for one month is prepaid by the medical insurance fund to drug distribution companies for the purpose of working capital, and the 30-day account period is strictly enforced.

However, under the Two-invoice System, circulation companies face the financial pressures from pharmaceutical manufacturers and the ultimate medical institutions. In case of the failure of recovery of accounts in time, circulation enterprises have to face the pressure of making advance payment, which is undoubtedly a major test for circulation enterprises. However, distributors with only channel promotion capabilities and without distribution capabilities will be eliminated and face the task of transition. In the process of industry consolidation, pharmaceutical wholesaling industry will have a serious competitive situation. Under the pressure of the competition, drug circulation companies have to adopt large-scale, commercialized, professional business development, improve its own management capability, and transform the means of business, thereby escaping the impact of market turmoil and industry consolidation.

2. Impact on marketing service-oriented enterprises

Under the Two-invoice System, small and medium-sized circulation enterprises face the transformation of business mode, and change from agency-type business to marketing service-oriented enterprises. The Two-invoice System and the Business Tax Replaced with Value-added Tax policy cut off the pharmaceutical circulation links, leading to standardized industry and better industry concentration. Wholesaling companies that chiefly engage in "business featuring the improper use of invoice issued by the pharmaceutical enterprise" or illegal sale of invoice will exit the industry. The traditional business model and finance and tax treatment model are unable to meet the requirements of the industry under the new system, and the business model must be reshaped. Agents with GSPs that cannot evolve into distributors have to become contract sales organizations (CSOs) specialized in marketing activities. Drug manufacturers and CSO sign a commission service agreement, and pay the consideration according to the agreement. By reshaping the new business model, pharmaceutical companies and CSOs establish legitimate and compliant service relationships to reduce the fiscal and tax risks in the pharmaceutical distribution. For agents, the original first-tier and large-scale regional agents will continue to expand their network of channels to improve coverage and consolidate control over terminal resources. There are many possibilities for the future transformation of agents at the second-tier and below, or enterprises become first-level agents through negotiation with manufacturers or become its sales outsourcer through acquisition by first-level agents, or are transformed into distributors. In the process of transformation, manufacturers must make reasonable choice of agents and establish new cooperative relations according to the characteristics of their own products, the distribution of target hospitals and costs, etc. The agents shall negotiate with the manufacturers about the division of responsibility for channels based on their own capabilities and future development plans to ensure the maximum interests.

3. 案例：国药控股应对“两票制”的主要策略

（1）强化进口

布局全国多仓第三方物流服务，从疫苗开始，应对局部地区出现的“一票制”要求。上海、北京和广州的进口布局，为进口药全国独家代理做相应准备。

（2）推动非“两票制”区域销售

加强零售业务建设，除国大药房之外鼓励各地分公司开设各种类型药店。提出“发展零售，服务零售”战略，促进传统调拨业务转型。

（3）营销推广业务

建立终端营销推广团队，同时包括医院和药店市场。充分借助总部和各地分公司的资源投入和合作。选择成熟、知名度高的品牌进行合作。

（4）引进保理业务

由国控上海先期尝试引入第三方保理，为原先采用底价代理的企业提供资金，利用供应商关系获得的品种优势，扩大各地医疗机构的合作能力。

“两票制”对药品流通企业的影响如图 8 所示。

大型流通	代理型商业	营销服务型
· 行业整合、覆盖面增加 · 成本增加，垫资压力增大 · 调拨业务收缩，纯销业务增加 · 对上下游议价能力增强 · 与工业间的商业合作模式受限	· 转型压力骤增（单向转往一级商） · 垫资功能弱化 · CRO 化（面向过专利期产品的 CSO 可能失去存在必要性的系统风险） · 非一级代理出局	· 医药第三方物流兴起、参与高值、高毛利业务 · 互联网因素介入，三证放开，直接配送“一票制”雏形 / B2B 电商 CSO/CSP 短期兴起，长期仍存在系统风险

图 8　“两票制”对药品流通企业的影响

3. Case: Sinopharm's main strategy to cope with the challenges brought about by the Two-invoice System

(1) Enhance the management of importation

It sets up the third-party logistics services featuring multiple warehouses across the country to cope with the requirements of the One-invoice System deployed in some regions, starting from vaccines. It makes preparations in Shanghai, Beijing and Guangzhou for becoming the exclusive agency in China for imported drugs.

(2) Promote sales in regions where the Two-invoice System is not launched

It strengthens to enhance its retail business. In addition to the Guoda Drug Stores, the company encourages branches around the country to set up various types of pharmacies, and puts forward the strategy of "developing and servicing retails" and promotes the transformation of its traditional internal transfer business.

(3) Marketing business

It sets up the end-user marketing team, targeting both hospitals and pharmacy stores. It uses the resources of the headquarters and branches to choose mature and well-known brands for cooperation.

(4) Introduction of the factoring business

It attempts to let Sinopharm Shanghai take the lead to introduce the third-party factoring business, providing capital to the manufacturing enterprises which previously adopted the floor price agency to make use their relations with the suppliers to obtain the advantageous varieties and expand its cooperation with the medical institutions across the country.

The impact of the Two-invoice System on pharmaceutical distribution companies is shown in Figure 8.

Large-scale commercial companies	Agency	Marketing services
· Industry consolidation, coverage increased · Increased costs, increased pressure of advance payment · Contraction of the internal transfer business, while increasing pure commercial business · The bargaining power with its upstream and downstream has been enhanced · Cooperation with the manufacturing industry is limited	· Surging pressure on transformation (one-way transition to become a level-1 agent) · Weakening the function of advance payment on behalf of others · CRO (Clinical Research Organization) [The systemic risk that contract sales organizations (CSO) may lose their necessity to exist for patent-expiring products] · Out-of-business of Non-level-1 agents	· Pharmaceutical third-party logistics are on the rise, to participate in high value, and high margin businesses · Internet factors involved, deregulation of three certificates, and prototype of the "one-invoice system" / B2B business which features direct delivery · CSOs / CSPs (commercial service providers) are on the rise in the short term, and there are still long-term systemic risks

Figure 8　Impact of the Two-invoice System on pharmaceutical distribution companies

（四）对传统经销商的影响

在底价代理模式下，传统的经销商、居间人正在尝试转型，急促承担原有角色。这些经销商转型的出路：被药企收编成为企业内部员工，或者与药企签订“推广”服务合同。随着税收监管趋紧，套取销售费用和资金周转问题成为这些经销商、居间人转型过程中的最大问题。从目前来看，大量经销商、居间人组建各类医药销售代理企业，以CSO、医药咨询公司等名义注册。这类企业通常为小微公司或注册于产业园区，尽可能利用国家相关税收优惠政策减免税收以提升利润空间并套取相关销售费用。

在“两票制”政策下，代理商将面临分类和重新选择。“两票制”后，医院和区域的代理商回到行业的起点：佣金制模式；随着代理商格局的演变，生产企业有必要系统性地进行代理商细分并从中挑选合适的代理商作为合作伙伴。这个过程中，生产企业需要全方位考虑竞争环境、合作关系、竞争战略等要素。

（五）对CSO等新兴组织的影响

在“两票制”形势下，当前的主流是由底价模式向佣金模式转变。药品生产企业自建推广队伍和CSO模式逐渐成为潮流。CSO作为专门从事市场推广活动的市场服务商，是通过外包将营销专业化的一种商业模式。“两票制”改革后，以往依靠“挂靠企业”“过票”等违规行为生存下来的大量的中小型企业，以及原来的代理商、中间商等市场中间参与者转变为在整个供应链上提供药品推广、营销和咨询的服务商。由于“两票制”改革下，流通环节的大幅缩减，药品流通模式由以往盛行的“低开”模式被迫逐步转变为“高开”。因营销模式的转型，中小型企业面临大规模的合并与重组，转型不成功的代理商将直接退出医药流通行业。成熟产品的省级代理存在的价值逐渐降低，分销模式有被强势的上游生产企业终结的风险；产品的销售资格、佣金的安全性和及时性、对上需要支付货款和回款、对下需要进行佣金的垫付，并且还有厂家对销售（医院覆盖、进销存数据）透明度的要求；佣金费用票据的提供难度加大，上游厂家、总代理商对票据的要求严苛，导致代理商利润进一步下降。

(IV) Impact on traditional dealers

Under the model of the floor price agency, traditional dealers and intermediaries are trying the transformation and quickly assume the original roles. The way out for these dealers is that they will become the internal staff of the pharmaceutical manufacturers into which they are incorporated, or sign a service contract for the promotion of medicines with the pharmaceutical enterprises. With the tightening of tax regulation, the misappropriation of sales expenses and the shortage of working capital have become the biggest problem for these distributors and intermediaries during their transformation. Currently, a large number of dealers and intermediaries have set up various types of pharmaceutical sales agencies and registered in the names of the CSOs or pharmaceutical consulting firms. These enterprises are usually small and micro businesses or register in industrial parks. They try to use relevant preferential tax policies of the State for tax exemptions and reductions, thus increasing profits and extracting relevant sales expenses.

In the context of the Two-invoice policy, agents will face re-classification and need re-origination. Hospitals and regional agents will go back to where they should be: the commission model. With the evolution of the agency models, manufacturers need to conduct a systematic breakdown of agents and select appropriate agents as partners. In this process, manufacturers need to consider broadly such factors as the competitive environment, cooperation, competition strategy and others.

(V) Impact on emerging organizations such as CSOs

Under the Two-invoice System, the current trend is shifting from the floor price model to the commission model. Drug manufacturers would build their own promotion teams, and the CSO model will gradually become the fashion. CSO is a marketplace service provider specialized in marketing activities, and is a business model in which such organizations provide the marketing services outsourced by manufacturers. After the reform of the Two-invoice System, a large number of small and medium-sized enterprises that have survived through the irregularities by means of license renting and other intermediate participants in the market such as the original agents and intermediaries will be transformed into service providers to provide services of drug promotion, marketing and consultation along the entire supply chain. Thanks to the Two-invoice System reform, the passing hands along the sales flow have been drastically reduced. And the pharmaceutical invoicing has been gradually transformed from the “low-invoicing” mode that was rampant in the past to the “high-invoicing” mode. Due to the transformation of the marketing mode, small and medium-sized enterprises are facing large-scale mergers and reorganizations, and those unsuccessful agents during the transition will be directly forced out from the pharmaceutical circulation industry. The provincial agencies with mature products will gradually shrink their value to exist, as their distribution model will face the risk to be terminated by the strong upstream production enterprises. The challenges that they encounter, such as sales qualification, commission security and timely delivery, the need to pay the purchase price, the need to give credits to their downstream partners, and the requirements to meet the sales transparency (hospital coverage, invoicing data) required by manufacturers, the increasing difficulty to provide commission fee bills, and the stringent requirements on the instruments by upstream manufacturers and general agents, all in all, will result in their profits to be further squeezed.

在“两票制”改革前，部分采用底价代理模式的药品生产企业低价销售药品给代理商，经过多环节经销，最终将药品高价销售给终端医疗机构。通过层层“过票”后最终将差价返还给生产企业。而在实行“两票制”后，仍存在部分“过票”套现的现象。同时，在“营改增”后，套现需解决开具真实“增值税发票”的问题。原有的部分不合规、被市场淘汰的中间代理商转型成 CSO。此类 CSO 成为提供营销、咨询等服务的第三方公司。事实上，依然有通过开具公司业务发票来“走票”“过票”的情况存在。

（六）对医疗机构的影响和政策应对延伸

“两票制” 并不能直接为医疗机构带来直接收益，医疗机构普遍希望避免因“两票制”带来的新增工作量和不必要风险。“两票制”亦非现代医院管理制度的组成部分，同时无助于临床质量提升，因此，很难成为医院最高管理层日常关注的重心内容。“两票制”的实施带来了大量的繁重验票核查工作，公立医院并无能力全面接管相关工作。为了有利于整顿药品流通市场，部分省市在建立“两票制”的同时，要求医院归并采购渠道，减少药品和耗材的供应商数量。以福建和安徽的经验来看，公立医院通常将验票职能转移到商业公司之中，由此使得商业公司因为应对验票核查而大幅增加日常工作量和经营成本。同时，由于政府财政投入不足，医院为了维持生存和发展，弥补医疗服务项目收不抵支的状况，就出现了多开药、开贵药、药价虚高的现象来弥补医疗服务亏损。而一些低价、质量好、性价比高的药品在这种状况下逐渐失去市场，反之贵药销量越来越高。这一现象的发生严重破坏了市场秩序，损害了公平有序的竞争环境。为了应对“两票制”引起的动荡，未来可能会有相关软件或 IT 技术来提升验票核查的能力。以福建的经验来看，渠道归并是当地主流商业公司的机遇。

在渠道组成中，渠道主体本质上就是各市场主要参与者，指流通渠道中从事流通经济活动的经济组织，既包括生产商、中间商和消费者等承担基本流通职能的主体，也包括承担各种辅助活动和功能的经济和服务机构。医药行业由于其特殊性受政府管控严重，在我国各参与主体的角色则受政府医改政策的影响而进行相应的变化调整。在“营改增”与“两票制”推行前，底价代理模式普遍，行业中承担流通职能的主体包括药品生产企业、代理商、商业公司和医院、药店等。2016 年，“营改增”与“两票制”政策推行后，底价代理模式难以为继，代理商纷纷转型，有药品经营资质的转

Before the Two-invoice System reform, some drug manufacturers adopted the f loor price agency model to sell to agents at low prices which, through many layers of middlemen, eventually sold products to the end users–medical institutions–at a high price. In this process through the hands and hands of "invoices passing" by illegal means of license renting, finally, the price difference will be paid to the manufacturer. After the Two-invoice System has been implemented, there still–to a less degree–exists the phenomenon of license renting for taking illegal cash. However, in the meantime, after the Business Tax Replaced with Value-added Tax, the agents need to issue a true Value-added Tax Invoice in order to make such income. The agents who were originally non-compliant and eliminated by the market could transform into CSOs. Such CSOs will become third-party companies that provide marketing, consulting and other services. In fact, there are still cases of "invoices passing" by illegal means of license renting.

(VI) Impact on medical institutions and policy responses

The Two-invoice System does not directly bring direct benefits to medical institutions. Medical institutions generally hope to avoid the additional workloads and unnecessary risks arising from the Two-invoice System. The Two-invoice System is also not an integral part of the modern hospital management system and does not necessarily help improve their clinic quality. It is therefore difficult to become a focus of hospitals' top management in their daily routine. The implementation of the Two-invoice System has resulted in a heavy workload of invoice check, and public hospitals may be not capable of taking over all the relevant works. In order to facilitate the rectification of the drug circulation market, some provinces and municipalities have set up the Two-invoice System and at the same time, require hospitals to merge purchasing channels and reduce the number of suppliers of pharmaceutical products and consumables. In the experience of Fujian and Anhui provinces, public hospitals usually transfer their invoice checking functions to commercial companies, thus resulting in significant increase of their daily workload and operating costs in regards to the invoice verification. At the same time, due to inadequate government subsidies and investment, in order to maintain their business and for further development, the doctors in the hospitals could prescribe more medicines for patients that are expensive to make up for medical service losses. As a result, while some low-cost, good-quality, cost-effective drugs in this situation would be gradually forced out of the market, the sales of expensive drugs are getting higher and higher. This phenomenon has seriously damaged the market order and undermined the fair and orderly competitive environment. In order to cope with the turmoil caused by the Two-invoice System, software or IT technologies may emerge in the future to enhance the ability of invoice checking and verification. In terms of the experience of Fujian province, channel consolidation is an opportunity for local mainstream commercial companies.

In the channel composition, the main players of channels are essentially the main participants in each segment of the market. They are economic organizations engaging in economic activities in the circulation channels, including producers, intermediaries and consumers that assume the basic functions of circulation, and also include economic and service agencies that assume the auxiliary activities and functions. Because of its particularity, the pharmaceutical industry is heavily regulated by the government. The role of the participants in the country as affected by the policy of medical reform of the government will make corresponding adjustments. Prior to the reform of the Business Tax

型为 CSO（合同销售组织）进行药品的销售推广，无资质但有服务能力的代理商则需转型为 CSP（商业性服务提供商），为工业企业提供市场调研、学术推广、技术咨询等各方面服务。因此，在目前这样的局面下，院内药品供应链业务日益获得公立医院的重视和青睐。

本质上来说，供应链业务是之前一直在各地发展的药房托管模式的升级版本。供应链模式最大的优势是将医院的以药品采购为核心的多个职能部门外包，形成向医院提供产品的服务链条，从而在其中获取收益。在民营资本托管的公立医院体系下，公立医院本身是非营利性的，供应链本身营利即可。但是，在目前公立医院自身希望自建或合作的供应链体系下，公立医院不仅将药房、采购和其他相关成本托付给供应链，还需要供应链公司按照一定的比例向其提供收益分成或固定上缴收益。这对公立医院来说，不仅可以暂时缓解药品零加成政策带来的收入下降压力，甚至可以由此获得更多收益。“两票制”政策的实施，在某种程度上推动了公立医院与强势主流商业流通企业合作，共同建设院内药品耗材供应链项目，从而固化医院与药品流通企业间的利益联系，甚至衍生出隐形以药补医。

（七）整个医药行业面临着重构竞争力的环境

1. 研发与生产

为提高医药产品品质，推动医药行业供给侧结构改革，应加大医药产业结构调整力度，加强技术创新。实施重大新药创制科技重大专项等国家科技计划，支持符合条件的企业和科研院所研发新药及关键技术，提升药物创新能力和质量疗效。推动落后企业退出，着力化解药品生产企业数量多、规模小、水平低等问题。支持药品生产企业兼并重组，简化集团内跨地区转移产品上市许可的审批手续，培育一批具有国际竞争力的大型企业集团，提高医药产业集中度。引导具有品牌、技术、特色资源和管理优势的中小型企业以产业联盟等多种方式做优做强。提高集约化生产水平，促进形成一批临床价值和质量水平高的品牌药。

replaced with Value-added Tax and the implementation of the Two-invoice System, the agency model at the floor price was common. The main players that undertook the circulation function in the industry included pharmaceutical manufacturers, agents, commercial companies, hospitals and pharmacies. After the implementation of the two policies since 2016, the agency model at the floor price has become irrelevant and unsustainable. Agents have to transform themselves, and some with qualification as pharmaceutical intermediary have transformed themselves into CSO (contract sales organization) to promote drug sales. However, some agents without the qualification but with the service capability need to transition to CSP (commercial service provider) in order for survival, to provide market research, academic promotion and technical advice services for industrial enterprises. Therefore, under the current situation, the hospital's pharmaceutical supply chain business has become increasingly welcomed by public hospitals.

In essence, the supply chain business is an upgraded version of the pharmacy hosting model that has been evolving across the country. The biggest advantage of the supply chain model is the outsourcing of hospitals' multiple departments with pharmaceutical procurement functions to form a service chain that provides products to the hospitals and thereby benefits them. Under the public hospital system managed by private capital, the public hospitals themselves are not for profit, and it is just okay that the supply chain itself can be profitable. However, currently in the context that public hospitals themselves want to build their own or cooperate to build supply chain system, they would not only like to entrust their pharmacies, purchases and other matters to the supply chain companies, but also wish the supply chain companies can return to them a certain percentage of revenue or a fixed number of the proceeds. For public hospitals, this will not only temporarily alleviate their pressure of declining income caused by the zero-markup policy, but may even result in more revenue for them. The implementation of the Two-invoice Policy has promoted the cooperation between public hospitals and strong mainstream commercial circulation enterprises to jointly build the supply chain for supplying hospital drug, so as to enhance the interest connection between them and even derive the compensation system for the medical cost through drug-selling profits.

(VII) The entire pharmaceutical industry is faced with the environment of competitiveness restructuring

1. R&D and production

In order to improve the quality of pharmaceutical products and promote the supply-side structural reform in the pharmaceutical industry, it should step up efforts to readjust the pharmaceutical industry structure and strengthen the technological innovation. It should implement national science and technology programs such as major scientific and technological projects for major new drug creation, and support qualified enterprises and research institutes to develop new drugs and key technologies to enhance the drug innovation capability and quality and efficacy. It should force out backward enterprises, and put efforts to resolve the problems of large number of small-scale and low-level drug manufacturers. It should support the merger and reorganization of drug manufacturing enterprises, simplify the examination and approval procedures for trans-regional transfer of products within a group, foster a batch of large-scale enterprise groups with international competitiveness, and enhance concentration of the pharmaceutical industry. And it should guide small and medium-sized enterprises that have the advantages in brands, technologies, special resources and management to become

2. 销售与营销

为了促进合理交流和临床水平提升，遏制打击商业贿赂。国务院办公厅印发《关于进一步改革完善药品生产流通使用政策的若干意见》，明确提出食品药品监管部门要加强对医药代表的管理，建立医药代表登记备案制度，备案信息及时公开。医药代表只能从事学术推广、技术咨询等活动，不得承担药品销售任务，失信的记入个人信用记录。

同时，我国药品流通环节多，流通秩序混乱，挂靠经营、过票洗钱、商业贿赂屡禁不止，推高了药品价格，腐蚀了医生队伍，诱导了大处方、开贵药，给国家、社会和个人造成很大的损失。对此现象国务院办公厅明确指出：为整治药品流通领域突出问题，食品药品监管、卫生计生、人力资源社会保障、价格、税务、工商管理、公安等部门要定期联合开展专项检查，严厉打击租借证照、虚假交易、伪造记录、非法渠道购销药品、商业贿赂、价格欺诈、价格垄断及伪造、虚开发票等违法违规行为，依法严肃惩处违法违规企业和医疗机构，严肃追究相关负责人的责任；涉嫌犯罪的，及时移送司法机关处理。健全有关法律法规，对查实的违法违规行为，记入药品采购不良记录、企事业单位信用记录和个人信用记录并按规定公开，公立医院两年内不得购入相关企业药品；对累犯或情节较重的，依法进一步加大处罚力度，提高违法违规成本，实施办法另行制定。

3. 分销与流通

为提高流通集中度，促进流通秩序规范，遏制流通环节出现“走票”“洗钱”问题。“营改增”的实行是让企业合理纳税的同时适当降低税负。统一执行增值税后，发票都进入同一增值税系统，可追溯性特别强，一个票号只对着一个流向，且行业间抵扣链条完整性凸显，偷税漏税很难，“过票”和“倒票”更难。以前可以冲账，但不能抵扣进项税的会议费、咨询费、广告费等，可以抵扣增值税款而降低实际的会议、咨询、广告成本。“营改增”之后，对于刚开始转型的底价代理制厂商来说，由于票务规范化，存在可抵扣的进项税有限、时间差等问题，其前期税负将大幅提高。

stronger with various ways such as industrial alliances, improve the level of intensive production, and promote the formation of a batch of branded medicines with high clinical value and quality.

2. Sales and marketing

In order to promote the rational exchange and improvement of clinical service, it should curb and fight against commercial bribery. The General Office of the State Council issued the *Opinions on the Further Reform and Improvement of the Policies to Be Used in the Production and Circulation of Medicines* which clearly states that the food and drug regulatory authorities shall strengthen the management of medical representatives and establish a registration system for medical representatives, and the record-keeping information shall be disclosed in a timely manner. Medical representatives can only engage in academic promotion, technical advice and other similar activities, and shall not assume the task of drug sales. And those who lost the credit shall be recorded in their personal credit history.

At the same time, there are many passing hands in the circulation of medicines in the country, and there are illegal affiliating, license renting and borrowing, money laundering and commercial bribery occured from time to time, which push up the prices of medicines, corrupt the doctors, and induce doctors to issue prescriptions with expensive medicines that cause great harm and losses to the country, society and individuals and result in a chaotic circulation market. The General Office of the State Council clearly pointed out: in order to solve the outstanding problems in the field of drug circulation, the food and drug regulatory authority, health department, family planning department, human resources department and social security ministry, as well as price, taxation, business administration, public security and other departments should conduct joint inspections on a regular basis, to strictly crack down on license renting, fake transactions, forging, illegal buying and selling drugs, commercial bribery, price fraud, monopoly and forgery, invoice falsifying and other illegal activities, and to severely punish illegal enterprises and medical institutions in accordance with the law and hold the relevant persons to responsibilities; and those who are suspected of crime should be promptly referred to the judiciary. And the relevant laws and regulations should be improved; for the illegal acts that are verified, they should be credited to the bad records of drug procurement, credit records of enterprises and institutions, and personal credit records, and publicized according to the regulations. In particularly, public hospitals shall not make purchase from such illegal companies within two years. For recidivism or heavier crime, it should further increase penalties according to the law and raise higher the costs of illegal activities, and formulate additional measures for implementation.

3. Distribution and circulation

In order to enhance the concentration of the circulation section and promote the standardization of the market, it should curb the problems of multiple passing-hands and money laundering. The implementation of the Business Tax replaced with Value-added Tax is to allow enterprises to pay reasonable taxes while appropriately reducing their tax burden. After the cross-board implementation of the unified value-added tax, all the invoices are the same VAT invoices, and its traceability is greatly enhanced. An invoice number flows only to one direction, and the tax deduction chain among different sectors gets much more improved. In such environment, tax evasion would be difficult, let alone license renting. The conference fees, consulting fees and advertising fees that previously can be offset in bookkeeping but cannot be deducted as input tax will decrease. However, after the

4. 供应链管理方面，物流、资金流和信息流建设仍需要进一步加强

医药行业供应链管理系统服务工程由两大部分组成，供应链管理应用系统和供应链管理服务，更形象一点的描述就是：供应链管理应用系统就是已修好的医药商品销售高速公路，供应链管理服务就是运营它的管理策略和收费服务站。其中，供应链管理应用系统也包括两个部分：第一部分是将传统管理的精华提炼出来，再融合先进的供应链管理理念开发的现代化大型医药配送中心的物流管理应用系统，它是支持医药行业供应链管理系统运行的基石，通过它完成了企业内部业务流程的一体化，从而使业务流程具有可监控性、资金流具有透明性、企业内外信息流具有共享性。在供应链管理系统中占有重要位置的各地区配送中心要靠这套系统联系起来，协同经营，支持电子商务系统的运行。

第二部分则是网上交易平台，是医药行业供应链管理系统核心的体现，最显著的特点有两个方面：先进管理理念指导下的精细化管理和强大信息处理系统的支持。有了这两点支撑，供应链中的每个环节都能及时利用最新和价值最高的相关信息来管理业务，实现产品从起点开始就以尽可能快的速度、最少的成本和更为完美的供需平衡流向最终的用户。

5. 稳定的渠道供应链管理体系

发票、货物、现金统一的物流体系管理，确保每一个医疗终端有必要的一级分销覆盖。在各地议价的环境下维护价格体系，能及时获得回款。“两票制”将改变企业物流体系，改变企业资金流管理。伴随物流和资金流的变化，企业需要更新信息系统，提供实施产品物流状态。

Business Tax replaced with Value-added Tax, the manufacturers who just start the transition from the floor price agency model will face a substantial increase in their tax burden due to such problems as standardization of invoicing, limited deducted input tax, and the time warp.

4. In terms of supply chain management, the construction for integration of goods flow, capital flow and information flow still needs to be further strengthened

The service program of the supply chain management system in the pharmaceutical industry consists of two parts, i.e. the supply chain management application system and the supply chain management service. A more vivid description is: the supply chain management application system is like a ready highway for pharmaceutical products sales, while the supply chain management service is like the management strategy and toll stations that run it. Of which, the application system also includes two parts. The first part is a logistics management application system of the modern large-scale pharmaceutical distribution center which is created based on the extracted traditional management essences and the modern advanced supply chain management concepts. It is a cornerstone that supports the operation of the pharmaceutical supply chain system, through which the business processes within an enterprise are integrated, so that making business processes be monitorable, financial flows transparent, and information flow be sharable. The regional distribution centers that occupy an important position in the supply chain management system rely on this system to interconnect, cooperate and support the operation of e-commerce systems.

The second part is the online trading platform, which reflects the core of the supply chain management system in the pharmaceutical industry. The most prominent feature is that it has two aspects: the fine management under the guidance of advanced management concepts and the support to powerful information processing system. With these two supports, every aspect of the supply chain can take advantage of the latest and most relevant information to manage the business in a timely manner, realizing the product flows to the end users as fast as possible, with least cost and with more perfect balancing of supply and demand from the starting point.

5. Stable channel supply chain management system

A logistics system management that integrates "invoice, goods, cash" ensures that each medical terminal has the necessary coverage of a level-1 distributor. Maintenance of the price system in the bargaining environment can timely secure payments. The Two-invoice System will change the enterprise logistics system, changing corporate cash flow management. With changes in logistics and cash flow, companies need to update their information systems to trace information of product logistics status.

八、亟待厘清或完善的重点问题

（一）两张票的认定问题

对两票的认定问题，目前各省出现了很多个性化的诉求：关于国内企业总代理的家数、总代理的身份性质如何确定；国内科工贸一体企业设立的商业公司、营销公司衍生出的一票；外企在国际上授权，进入国内后的转授权，持证人与国内代工企业不一致而增加的一票；外企与外企、外企与国内企业设立联合研发、生产、推广的产品，也可能额外增加出一票；外资在华工厂生产本地化产品，委托国内企业作为总代理，总代理向商业企业销售的情况。总代理这一票的认定与国内企业设立总代理这一票形式相似，具体应如何认定；外资在华全资贸易公司与进口一级代理商存在平行业务时应如何认定票据；全国性或跨省域大型商业企业设立的控股或全资分子公司所发生的票据（上下或横向及逆向发生的销售或调拨）应如何认定。关于在认定两张票的问题上各省存在的差异，还需进一步讨论与完善。

（二）验票问题

医疗机构验票存在巨大技术障碍。

首先，由于医药流通企业的商业本质是集货与分销，这个业务流程所产生的票据天然存在前后不对等的情形：商业企业从药品生产企业获得的发票是品种相对集中和数量较少但数额巨大的工业发票，总体数量有限，但开具给医院的发票则品种、规格众多，涉及厂商众多，批号众多的分散型发票。前后票据间不仅数量差异巨大，更重要的是，两张发票间的内容缺乏关联性，发票信息无法一一对应，无法证实发票和发货清单之间的联系。其次，在医院端，医院验票、采购平台验票时可能会出现发票无生产批号信息，无法证实发票与随货清单之间的关联，票据信息不完全，两票之间的关联性弱等问题。再次，医院既没有能力、也缺乏足够动力去进行“两票制”发票的查验工作。“两票制”验票问题的产生会加大医疗机构的人力、物力成本，进一步推动医院寻求药房托管甚至剥离，或者进一步强化医院进行药品耗材二次议价的动力。

VIII. Key issues that need to clarify or improve in the Two-invoice System

(I) Identification of two invoices

For the issue of identifying and confirming the two invoices, currently there are a lot of individual appeals from different provinces: the number of domestic general agents, and the identity nature of the general agents; an invoice that is issued by commercial companies / marketing companies that are set up by domestic scientific research and trade and manufacturing conglomerate enterprises; an invoice that incurred due to international authorization and domestic sub-delegation of foreign enterprises, and that the holder of authorization certificate is not the same as the domestic contracted manufacturers; an invoice may be issued by a JV set up by foreign companies and foreign enterprises or by foreign enterprises and domestic enterprises that engage in R&D, promotion and production; an invoice may occur in case of that foreign-funded factories in China produce localized products and commission domestic enterprises as the general agent which make sales to commercial enterprises. The invoice of the general agent is similar to the invoice that the general agent set up by domestic enterprises. How to identify it? When foreign funded wholly-owned trading companies have a parallel business with their level-1 importer agent in China, how to identify the invoice? An Invoice (sales or transfers or reverse sales) may occur by a controlled or wholly owned subsidiary established by a nationwide or inter-provincial large-scale commercial enterprise, and then how to identify it? The discrepancies among the provinces in identifying two invoices need to be further discussed and clarified.

(II) The issue of checking invoice

There is a huge technical barrier for medical institutions to check invoice.

First of all, since the commercial nature of pharmaceutical distribution enterprises is the collection and distribution of goods, the invoices generated by this business process are inherently unequal: the invoices obtained by commercial enterprises from pharmaceutical manufacturing enterprises are relatively concentrated in variety and relatively small in number but huge in quantity. However, the invoices issued to the hospitals are involving more in goods varieties, specifications, more manufacturers, and more scattered invoices. Not only there are huge differences in the number of bills before and after a sale, but more importantly, the contents of the two invoices generated along the sales route may lack of relevance, the invoice information cannot be corresponding from one to one, and it is unable to confirm the relations between invoice and shipping list. Second, at the hospitals end, when the hospitals or purchase platforms check invoice, it may emerge the problems that invoices are without the lot number information, and it is unable to confirm the association between the invoices and the shipping list. As the bill information is not complete, the relation between bills is weak. Third, the hospitals have neither the capacity nor sufficient incentive to carry out the inspection of the Two-invoice System. The issue of invoice inspection under the Two-invoice System will increase the costs, manpower and material resources of medical institutions, further promote the institutions to search for the pharmacy hosting model or even divest the pharmacy, or further strengthen their impetus for the second bargaining of medical supplies.

税票作为“两票制”政策实施的载体与核心，有效地对其信息进行甄别，是该政策顺利实施的关键。因此，充分调动税务部门的积极性，参与到税票的稽查工作中来显得尤为重要。在实施“两票制”政策之前的多轮药品流通治理整顿行动中，纪检监察部门和药监部门也曾将“走票”“洗钱”列为重点治理整顿对象，但收效甚微。原因之一就是票据管理需要有专业的税务稽查能力，而纪检监察部门和药监部门在治理整顿行动中未能得到税务部门的有效支持。同时，公立医疗卫生机构作为“两票制”政策的具体落实单位，必须核实药品批发企业从生产企业采购的发票，对票据涉及的量、批次等详细信息进行核对。而在电子发票尚未全面实行的条件下，确保商流、物流、信息流和票据的一致，对医疗卫生机构的财务工作人员的税票甄别能力和承受能力无疑是一项挑战。公立医疗卫生机构在争取税务部门支持的同时，也需要增强自身的财务管理能力。

从目前在浙江、湖南和上海的实践来看，“两票制”验票问题的解决出路似乎在于交由药品集中采购平台来进行验票。药品生产、流通及配送企业在发生相应购销业务时，通过电子化票据上传等手段，将“两票制”所涉及的各类票据信息提交给省市公共资源交易机构的药品采购平台，实施集中验票。由此来降低药品供应和使用各主体的社会交易和管理成本。

（三）“两票制”政策产生额外的社会经济成本

1. 医疗机构终端验票成本

因为“两票制”要求医疗机构在药品验收入库时，要核对药品流通企业提供的生产企业开出的进货发票复印件，做到票、账、货、款一致，这些核对票据的要求进一步增加了医疗机构药房的工作负担，部分医疗机构的药房已经转变为成本部门，不再有营利空间，因而“两票制”的实施使得药房还要梳理核对药品生产企业开给流通企业的发票，将进一步增加人力成本。

2. 工商企业经营模式转型的沉淀和沉没成本

工业企业增设一级商的运营管理成本增加。“两票制”后，出于压缩流通环节需要，所有二级、三级代理 / 流通商都升级为一级代理商，对药企来说，将面对管理众多一级客户的难题。营销管理难度加大，因一级配送商业数量大大增加，渠道管理难度也

As a base stone in implementation of the Two-invoice System, tax receipt that can effectively discriminate their information is the key to smoothly implement the policy. Therefore, to fully mobilize the enthusiasm of the tax department to participate in the inspection of tax receipts shows particularly important. In the rounds of crack-down and rectification of bad behaviors in the pharmaceutical circulation prior to the implementation of the Two-invoice System, the discipline inspection and supervision departments and drug administration departments have also listed "licence renting" and "money laundering" as key objects for crack-down and rectification, but it produces little effect. One of the reasons is that bill management requires professional tax inspection capabilities. But the discipline inspection and supervision departments and drug administration departments failed to get the effective supports from the taxation authorities during the rectification. At the same time, as required to concretely implement the policy of the Two-invoice System, public medical institutions must verify the invoices purchased by the pharmaceutical wholesale enterprises from the manufacturing enterprises, and check the detailed information about the quantities and batches involved in the bills. Under the current condition that the electronic invoice has not yet been fully available, to ensure consistency between business flow, logistics, information flow and bills, it is undoubtedly a daunting challenge to the screening ability and affordability of the financial staff of medical and health institutions. While seeking support from tax departments, public health agencies also need to enhance their financial management capabilities.

From the current practices in Zhejiang, Hunan and Shanghai, the solution to the problem of invoice check in the Two-invoice System appears lying on the platforms of centralized medicine procurement. When drug producers, distributors and logistic companies conduct purchases and sales, they may through uploading the electronic bills and other means submit various types of paper information to the drug procurement platforms managed by provincial and municipal public resource trading institutions for the implementation of the centralized check and verification, thus reducing the social transaction and management costs of the supply and use of medicines.

(III) Additional social and economic costs generated under the Two-invoice System

1. Costs of checking invoice by medical institutions

Because the Two-invoice System requires medical institutions to check the copies of the purchase invoices during the storage of drugs that pharmaceutical distribution companies purchased from manufacturers to ensure the consistency between invoices, accounts, goods, and payments, these requirements further increase the workload of pharmacies of medical institutions, and make some pharmacies in some medical institutions just become "a cost department" with no room for profiting. So, as the implementation of the Two-invoice System makes the pharmacies have to sort out and check the invoices issued by the pharmaceutical manufacturing enterprises to the circulation enterprises, this will further increase labor costs.

2. Precipitation and sunk costs during the transformation of the business models of the industrial and commercial enterprises

The operation and management cost of the tier-one agents set by by industrial enterprises will increase. After the Two-invoice System is implemented, out of the requirements to compress the

随之加大；公司内部对合规的要求超过以往，财务、营销、合规部门将三足鼎立。商务、合规等管理成本增加，与过去相比较，行业的营销效率将下降。

工业和流通企业垫资成本、多级代理体系瓦解带来垫资集中化。由于“两票制”下配送商的数量遭到限制，在有限的配送商之间，少量的配送商逐渐占据了市场垄断地位，导致商业回款周期延长。同时，企业被迫调整销售和财务结构，需要在“营改增”和金税系统监管下做到费用结构合理且规范，没有原先“过票”公司的垫资，存在一定资金压力和应收账款风险。上述成本最终将转化为社会成本并以药价形式体现。

（四）各省（区、市）实施“两票制”的进度不一、总体较慢

在《印发关于在公立医疗机构药品采购中推行“两票制”的实施意见（试行）的通知》（国医改办发〔2016〕4号）出台之前，不少省（区、市）就开始了对“两票制”的探索。医改标杆省份安徽率先垂范，自2016年11月起就在省内所有公立医疗机构推开“两票制”。11个医改省（区、市）中，除福建外，安徽、陕西、青海、重庆均发布了正式版的“两票制”实施意见。但从目前医改试点省（区、市）“两票制”的进展情况看，江苏、浙江、上海“两票制”推行滞后尤其值得关注。

（五）医改政策引起的利益相关者行为调整带来严重的产业调整

目前，我国医药行业大型企业数量占少数，大多数企业规模都不大。实行“两票制”后，虽市场在逐渐朝着集约化的态势发展，但这之间还有很长的一段路要走。除非法经营的企业被淘汰出局外，存活下来的中小型医药企业的生存空间也会变得更加狭小，竞争会变得更加激烈，另外，“两票制”“营改增”等政策的发布必会使得各利益相关方采取一系列的应对措施，由此可能会引发医药批发行业的动荡。

circulation chain, all secondary and tertiary agents / distributors have to be upgraded to level-1 agents, so for the pharmaceutical manufacturing companies, they will face the challenge of managing a large number of level-1 customers. Because of a large increase in the number of level-1 agents, sales and marketing management becomes more difficult, so as the channel management. Internally in a company, as the compliance requirements are more demanded than ever, the compliance department will rise in par with the finance and marketing departments. Business, compliance and other management costs would increase, and compared with the past, the industry's marketing efficiency will decline.

The advance payments by manufacturing and circulation enterprises paying on behalf of partners will be densely converged due to the collapse of the multilevel agency system. As the number of distributors under the Two-invoice System is limited, a small number of distributors would gradually occupy the market monopoly status, resulting in lengthy extension of the commercial payment cycle. At the same time, enterprises are forced to adjust the sales and financial structure. They need to make their cost structure reasonable and standardized under the regulations of the Bussiness Tax Replaced with Value-added Tax and the golden tax system. As there is no advancement capital contribution from the original "license renting" companies, they could encounter certain financial pressures and the risk of accounts receivable. The above costs will eventually be translated into social costs and reflected in the form of drug prices.

(IV) The progress made by different provinces (autonomous regions and municipalities) in implementing the Two-invoice System varies and is generally slower

Before the releasing of the *Notice on the Printing and Distribution of the Implementation Opinions on the Two-invoice System to Be Adopted in the Drug Procurement of Public Medical Institutions* (*for trail implementation*) (GYGBF〔2016〕No. 4), many provioces (autonomous regions and municipalities) had begun their exploration of the Two-invoice System. Anhui, a medical reform model province, took the lead to launch the Two-invoice System in all public medical institutions in November 2016. Except for Fujian, among the 11 medical reform provinces (autonomous regions and municipalities), Anhui, Shaanxi, Qinghai and Chongqing all released the opinions on implementing official versions of the Two-invoice System. However, if we see the progress of implementing the Two-invoice System in the pilot provinces (autonomous regions and municipalities), it is particularly noteworthy that the implementations in Jiangsu, Zhejiang and Shanghai still lag behind.

(V) The adjustment of stakeholder behaviors caused by the medical reform policy would cause massive industrial restructuring

At present in China's pharmaceutical industry, large-scale enterprises accounts for a small percentage, and most are not large entities. Although the market is gradually moving toward the trend of intensive development after the implementation of the Two-invoice System, there is still a long way to get to the goal. Unless the illegal businesses are eliminated, the living space of the survived small and medium-sized pharmaceutical enterprises will be further squeezed. The competition will become more fierce. In addition, the promulgation of the policies such as the Two-invoice System and the Business Tax Replaced with Value-added Tax will inevitably lead to stakeholders to take a series of response measures, which may trigger turmoil in the pharmaceutical wholesale industry.

（六）“两票制”尚待解决的问题

一是“两票制”在推行初期只覆盖部分地区，还不能完全解决药品层层推销代理的问题，药品带金销售的问题可能不会很快消失。“多级代理”“非法挂靠”“过票洗钱”的空间将会进一步被挤压，但短期内不会完全消失，治理药品价格虚高的现象暂时不会取得最佳成效。

二是在推行“两票制”过渡期间，可能会对部分低价药品、用量小的药品的供应带来一些影响。由于这些药品生产企业不愿零散销售，配送企业大量采购之后因销售量有限，面临过期失效、经济损失等问题，可能会影响到供应。为此，我们要求流通企业按照远近结合、城乡联动的原则，做到区域药品配送城乡一体化，打通乡村药品配送“最后一公里”。各地也可通过要求流通企业在配送用量大、利润高药品的同时，配送那些用量小、价格低的药品，以总体保证利润平衡和市场供应。

三是推行“两票制”可能会受到以代理、过票等为主要业务的部分企业的反对和阻挠。“两票制”改革的推进将快速提升行业集中度，很多地区的中、小型药品流通企业将面临淘汰，逐渐形成全国统一的大市场。然而，部分省、市、县政府仍然单纯从促进辖区经济发展的角度出发，通过行政命令形式限制竞争，削弱药企跨地域兼并重组的动力，放缓资源整合升级和优化的步伐。如医疗卫生机构的药品招标采购，各地方政府政策往往倾向于给本地药品生产企业和流通企业更多的市场份额；另外，地方政府在医药企业的跨地域并购中常常设置阻碍等。同时，伴随着“营改增”税务系统的全面改制推进，地方税收锐减，地税出现结构性断层，对地方税务和财政收入的稳定增长提出严峻挑战。而“两票制”政策的实施意味着部分制药工业和商业不发达的地市级、县级区域征税企业数量被压缩，直接导致地方政府执行“两票制”政策的意愿下降或另行设置行政壁垒。药品流通企业不得不在每一重要地市都设立子公司，不利于提高运行效率。以国药集团为例，该集团拥有 300 多张《药品经营质量管理规范》认证证书和《药品经营许可证》，基本在每个地级市区域都成立了独立法人的子公司缴纳税款，若不如此就无法获得当地政府的土地使用批文，使大集团公司被强制拆分，与提升行业集中度的改革方向背道而驰。目前，我国破除地方保护主义尚任重

(VI) Problems to be solved in the Two-invoice System

First, the Two-invoice System only covers parts of the country in the initial stage of the implementation. It cannot yet completely solve the problem of multi-layer drug sales agents. The problem of "multilevel agency", "illegal license renting" and "money-laundering" will be further squeezed, but may not disappear in the short term. And the effort to root out of the phenomenon of too-high drug prices will not achieve the best results for the time being.

Second, during the transitional period of implementing the Two-invoice System, it may bring some impacts on the supply of some low-price medicines and some less-user medicines. As the pharmaceutical manufacturers producing such medicines are not willing to retail, so those distribution companies have to store a large number of such medicines and could face the risks of medicine expire and economic losses due to the insufficient sales that may affect the supply. To this end, we urge the circulation enterprises to achieve the integration of urban and rural medicine distributions in accordance with the principle of caring both rural and remote areas, so as to deliver medicines to the most remote villages. Locals may also require distribution companies while distributing pharmaceuticals with large amount of users and high profits, to distribute medicines with less users and low prices, to ensure the overall profit balance and market supply.

Third, the implementation of the Two-invoice System may be opposed and obstructed by some enterprises whose principal business is acting as agent with license renting. The promotion of the reform of the Two-invoice System will rapidly raise the industry concentration. A large number of small and medium-sized drug circulation enterprises in regions will face the risk of elimination as the market will gradually form a national unified big market. However, some provincial, municipal and county governments still limit competition by means of administrative orders as they simply consider promoting regional economic development of their own jurisdictions, thus weakening the motivation of pharmaceutical companies to make cross-regional mergers and acquisitions and slowing the pace of resource integration, upgrading and optimization. For example, in a drug bidding event held by local medical institutions, local governments tend to give bigger market shares to local drug manufacturers and distribution companies. In addition, they often set obstacles to inter-regional mergers and acquisitions of medical companies. At the same time as the overall tax is restructuring and the Business Tax Replaced with Value-added Tax is implemented, local taxes reduce drastically, and the structure failure of the local government tax poses severe challenges to the steady growth of local tax revenue and fiscal revenue. In addition, the implementation of the Two-invoice System policy means that the number of tax-paying enterprises in some prefecture-level cities and county-level regions where the pharmaceutical manufacturing and distribution industries are underdeveloped would be undercut greatly, which directly results in the unwillingness of local governments to implement the Two-invoice System, or otherwise they would set administrative barriers. So, drug distribution companies have to set up subsidiaries in each important city that is not conducive to improving operational efficiency. Taking Sinopharm Group as an example, the group owns more than 300 certificates certified under the *Management Practice of Medicine Operating Quality* and the *License of Pharmaceutical Trading*, and sets up subsidiaries of independent legal status nearly in each prefecture-level city to pay local taxes, rather than setting up branches. If it didn't do this, it could not obtain the local government's approval

道远，对滥用行政手段限制竞争的行为还需顶层设计随着逐渐全面推行“两票制”，对整顿药品流通秩序、完善行业监管都有着积极的影响。随着近几年来国家推行“两票制”的浪潮越来越激烈，不由得引发一些专业人士对大力推广“两票制”的疑惑。政府以强硬的行政手段进行干预是否会无法与如今市场化的经济活动相适应、是否会遭到原本利益既得者的抵触。

for land use. This forced the large group companies to be forced to be split, which runs counter to the direction of the reform to enhance industry concentration. At present, there is still a long way to go to get rid of local protectionism in our country, and it is required top-level design to limit the abuse of administrative measures that limits competition. With the gradual and full implementation of the Two-invoice System, it will have a positive influence on rectification of abnormal drug circulation and improvement of industry regulation. While in the increasingly fierce wave of implementing the state-sponsored Two-invoice System in recent years, some professionals have been tempted to stir up doubts about vigorously promoting the Two-invoice System. Whether the government intervenion with hard-line administrative measures is unable to adapt to the current market-oriented economic activities, and whether it will be resisted by the people with vested interests.

九、政策建议

通过上述研究，笔者提出下列建议。

（1）政府有关部门应明晰药品购销“两票制”的政策定位。药品购销“两票制”政策不仅仅是一个着眼于破除药品价格虚高、降低药品价格和费用、防止药品购销活动中发生商业贿赂和不道德影响、推动药品流通行业整合的医改政策；它同时也是一项非常重要的财税政策：通过购销“两票制”和金税工程的协同作用，通过规范药品生产企业的财税行为，从源头上清除“挂靠”“走票”的机制与空间，从源头根治药品购销活动中发生商业贿赂的财务根基；它更是一项全面、重新安排药品生产流通格局的产业政策：“两票制”政策重构了药品价值链在全生命周期、全环节的空间分配，重新定义药品生产和流通在价值链中的行业位置与比重，服务于医药卫生整体事业的社会目标。

（2）“两票制”政策可以借鉴药品供给侧治理改革的有益经验。药品社会规制领域所推动的供给侧治理改革，核心理念在于强化药品生产企业在药品全生命周期管理中的责任主体地位，让药品生产企业作为药品市场准入的责任主体、在生产流通使用全过程中的药品质量管理与风险控制责任主体、营销行为责任主体和价格行为责任主体。药品购销“两票制”政策的施行，让生产企业成为药品购销活动的责任主体、财税行为主体和价格及合规活动主体，更有利于实现药品全生命周期管理过程中明确归责原则，推动药品生产企业选择合适的营销模式和推广行为，从而规范其价格行为。

（3）药品购销“两票制”政策的核心理念在于强化药品持证人关键责任主体角色。通过明确归责的原则，约束身为重资产部门的药品持证人（生产企业）的行为。让持证人选择合适的营销模式、销售渠道和配送方式满足监管要求；自觉按照法规、政策要求约束价格行为，从而实现行业自律、企业行为回归（图9）。

IX. Policy recommendations

Based on the above research, the following recommendations are put forward.

(1) The relevant government departments should make a clear policy orientation of the Two-invoice System of pharmaceutical circulation. The policy of the Two-invoice System in the purchase and sales of medicines is not merely a policy of medical reform that focuses on breaking up the vicious cycle of high price medicines, reducing medicare prices and costs, preventing commercial bribery and immoral effects in the purchase and sale of drugs, and promoting the integration of the drug circulation industry, but is also a very important fiscal and taxation policy: it will be through the synergy between the Two-invoice System and the Golden Tax Project and the standardization of the fiscal and taxation activities of pharmaceutical manufacturing enterprises to eliminate the mechanism and space of "licence renting" and "tax evasion" and eradicate bribery in the purchase and sales of drugs from the source. It is also a comprehensive industrial policy that reschedules pharmaceutical production and circulation: the policy of the Two-invoice System reconstructs the space distribution of the pharmaceutical value chain in the entire life cycle and the whole process, and redefines the status of medicine production and distribution in the value chain in the industry, to serve the overall cause of medical and social goals.

(2) The Two-invoice System can learn from the beneficial experiences of drug supply-side governance reform. In the supply-side governance reform promoted in the pharmaceutical regulation field, the core concept lies in strengthening the leading position of pharmaceutical manufacturers in the whole life-cycle management of pharmaceuticals, making pharmaceutical manufacturers become the main players among players accessed to the drug market, the main players responsible for drug quality management and risk control in the whole process of production and distribution, the main players responsible for product marketing, and the main players responsible for pricing behavior. In addition, the implementation of the Two-invoice System allows manufacturing enterprises to become the main players responsible for drug purchasing and marketing activities, the main players responsible for paying taxation, and the main players responsible for pricing compliance, and it would be more conducive to realizing the principle of clearly defining responsibilities in the whole life-cycle management of medicines and promoting the medicine manufacturers to choose the right marketing model and promotion activities, so as to regulate their price behavior.

(3) The core concept of the Two-invoice System of pharmaceutical circulation lies in strengthening the key responsibility and the role of the marketing authorization holders. It is through the principle of clearly defining responsibilities to constrain the act of the marketing authorization holders (manufacturing enterprise) which generally have heavy assets, to enable the licensees to select the appropriate marketing model, sales channels and delivery methods that meet the regulatory requirements; and consciously in accordance with laws and regulations and policy requirements, to restrain pricing behavior, so as to achieve industry self-displine and compliant corporate behaviors (Figure 9).

(4)“两票制”政策的顺利推行，需要确立政府干预、市场调节的边界，政府相关部门应当为“两票制”政策进行清晰的概念界定和制定相关利益主体行为规范指南，同时尽力依靠市场作为配置资源的基础机制，在实现政府合理、有限干预的前提下，积极推动行业自律建设，最终通过道德规范、行业准则和企业自律来实现行为治理。通过科技创新、管理创新来降低由于“两票制”的施行所增加的非必要社会交易成本，最终能让药品价格和行业治理的政策惠及民生。

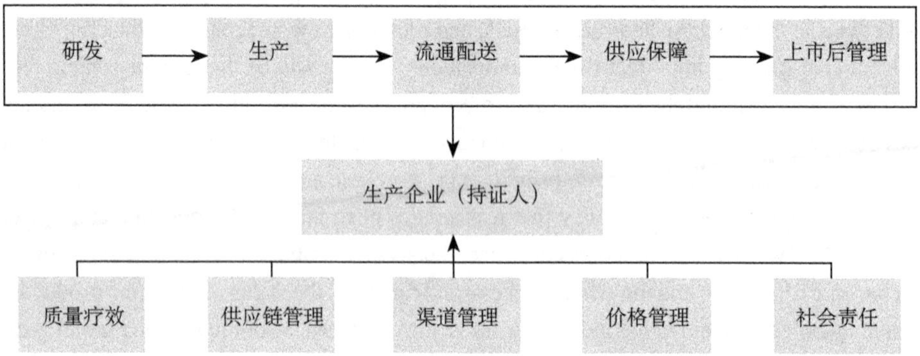

图 9　突出生产企业在药品生命周期管理中的关键责任主体角色

药品购销“两票制”政策的核心理念亦在于：让持证人选择合适的营销模式、销售渠道和配送方式满足监管要求；自觉按照法规、政策要求约束价格行为，从而实现行业自律、企业行为回归。

(4) To successfully implement the Two-invoice System policy, it requires the establishment of a boundary between government intervention and market regulation. The relevant government departments should clearly define the concepts of the Two-invoice System and formulate guidelines to regulate the conduct of relevant stakeholders, while best relying on the market as a basic mechanism to allocate resources. It should be based on the premise of reasonable and limited intervention of the government, to actively promote self-discipline of the industry and ultimately achieve behavior management through ethics, industry standards and corporate self-regulation. It should be through science and technology innovation and management innovation, to reduce the unnecessary social transaction costs incurred due to the implementation of the Two-invoice System, to ultimately enable the policies of pharmaceutical prices and industry governance to benefit people's livelihood.

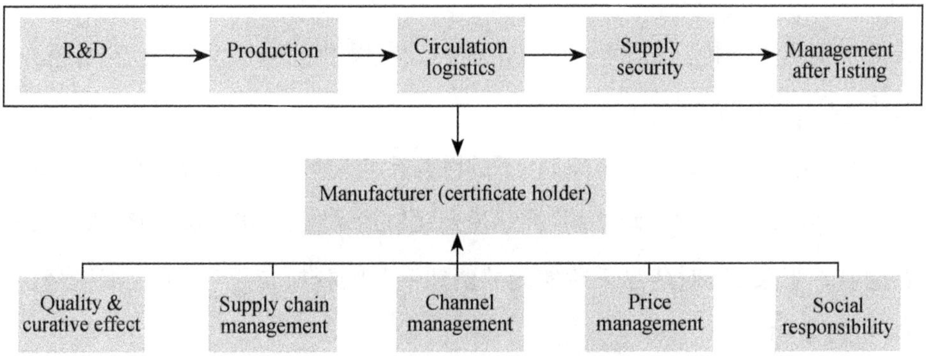

Figure 9 Highlight the key roles of manufacturers in the life cycle management

The core concept of the Two-invoice System of pharmaceutical circulation lies in: enable the licensees to select the appropriate marketing model, sales channels and delivery methods that meet the regulatory requirements; and consciously in accordance with laws and regulations and policy requirements, to restrain pricing behavior, so as to achieve industry self-discipline and compliant corporate behaviors.

参考文献

[1] 药品现代流通课题组 . 药品现代流通研究报告 [M]. 北京：中国经济出版社，2010.

[2] 王雪莹，雷晓盛 .“两票制”对各利益相关者的影响 [J]. 管理观察，2017（3）：75-77.

[3] 张帆，王帆，侯艳红 .“两票制”下药品供应链的重塑和发展 [J]. 卫生经济研究，2017（4）：11-15.

[4] 王国强 . 浅议“营改增”+“两票制”下的医药行业转型发展 [J]. 投资与创业，2017（8）.

[5] 黄河，孙静，刘远立 .“两票制”药品流通领域改革探讨 [J]. 中国药房，2017，28（18）.

[6] 黄丽君，干荣富 . 对药品采购实施“两票制”的分析与思考 [J]. 上海医药，2016，37（17）：61-63.

[7] 许方霄，高军 .“两票制”的路途不会平坦 [J]. 首都食品与医药，2016，23（15）：26-27.

[8] 丁锦希，田然，陈烨，等 .“两票制”政策下我国药品配送模式研究 [J]. 中国卫生政策研究，2017，10（6）：1-5.

[9] 国务院办公厅 . 关于印发《深化医药卫生体制改革 2016 年重点工作任务的通知》[EB/OL].（2016-04-26）[2019-01-20]. http://www.gov.cn/zhengce/content/2016-04/26/content_5068131.htm.

[10] 国君医药研究报告 [Z].

[11] 联讯证券研究报告 [Z].

[12] 姜天一 . 三明：“两票制”堵住加价漏洞 [J]. 中国卫生，2016（5）：19-20.

[13] 覃拥 . 新政引发医药商业物流变革 [J]. 物流技术与应用，2016，21（8）：64-67.

[14] 张馨月，雷寒 . 药品供应链管理的现状、问题及 JIT 模式 [J]. 中国医院药学杂志，2013，33（2）：152-154.

[15] 罗晶晶 . 治理药价虚高需要“晒”[N]. 中国会计报，2016-04-22（001）.

[16] 彭向辉 . 我国医药供应链现状及成因分析 [J]. 物流技术，2007，26（6）：91-93.

[17] 史丽丽 . 药品供应链现状分析 [J]. 价值工程，2011，30（36）：10-11.

[18] 李格林 . 医药电商模式对我国医药供应链的优化作用分析 [J]. 中国卫生信息管理杂志，2015（3）：304-307.

[19] 谢丽云，段利忠，卢奇，等 . 基于我国药品流通模式的供应链优化创新研究 [J]. 中国药房，2014（29）：2692-2695.

[20] 福建省商务厅市场秩序处 . 福建省药品流通行业发展现状和政策建议 [EB/OL].（2014-12-31）[2019-01-20]. http://www.fiet.gov.cn/xxgk/dybg/201501/t20150104_143475.htm.

[21] 福建省外经贸厅 .2015 年福建省药品流通行业情况 [EB/OL].（2016-03-03）[2019-01-20]. http://fujian.mofcom.gov.cn/article/sjgongzuody/201603/20160301267303.shtml.

[22] 盛平，冯艺文，卢海雄 . 试论药品采购“两票制”[J]. 中国现代药物应用，2008，2（2）：109-111.

[23] 国务院办公厅 . 关于完善公立医院药品集中采购工作的指导意见（国办发〔2015〕7 号）[EB/OL].（2015-02-09）[2019-01-20]. http://www.gov.cn/zhengce/content/2015-02/28/content_9502. htm.